Who Cried for The Little Girl

By
Andrea E. Clark

Copyright © 2013 by Andrea E. Clark

Who Cried For The Little Girl
by Andrea E. Clark

Printed in the United States of America

ISBN 9781626971721

All rights reserved solely by the author. The author guarantees all contents are original and do not infringe upon the legal rights of any other person or work. No part of this book may be reproduced in any form without the permission of the author. The views expressed in this book are not necessarily those of the publisher.

Unless otherwise indicated, Bible quotations are taken from the New King James Version (NKJV). Copyright © 1982 by Thomas Nelson, Inc. Used by permission. All rights reserved.

www.xulonpress.com

❦❀❧

"And we know that all things work together for the good of those who love God and are called according to His purpose" –Romans 8:28.

Acknowledgements

For booking information: Andrea Clark, P.O. Box 504, Lathrop, CA 95330

Email: ladyaclark@yahoo.com

Clothing & Accessories provided by: Jesus Rocks!! www.jesusrocks.biz

Hair and Make up: Adesuwa Idehen @ Moods & Attitudes Too 420 15th Street, Oakland, CA

EDITED BY: Dr. Lily Jenkins & UpgradeU Editing Services (Atlanta, GA), 1-888-354-9970 Ext. 3, http://www.keystothekingdomcoaching.com/upgradeu.html

Book cover design by : Vanessa Miller (775)412-2300 nessalynn77@gmail.com

Dedication

I dedicate this book to my beloved son, Rodney Demetrie Lampkin Jr.

Son, I love you so much. You literally mean the world to me. There's not a day that goes by that I don't think about you. I wanted to complete this book so that you would one day be able to say, "Wow, my mom really wrote a book." I wanted something for you to remember me by. I wanted to do something that would make you proud to be my son. But even more importantly, I wanted something that would allow you to know that no matter what life brings you, God will always give you a way of escape. So I say to you, son, learn from the things I have spoken to you and from my story in this book. In essence, real success comes from God.

Love you son.

Table of Contents

Nightmares on 34th Avenue 11
Growing Pains 15
So You Think You're a Woman Now 29
Baby Mama Drama 39
I Do, Again 49
Who Cried for the Little Girl? 61
Romans 8:28 73

Chapter 1

Nightmares on 34th Avenue

🙠 ✿ ⊱

It's 4:00 a.m., September 12, 1996, and I have awakened again from a bad dream. I'm about six years old and my hair is in two ponytails with white ribbons. I have on a white cotton gown with a black and white checker-printed robe. I'm lying on a pink carpet on the bathroom floor. My head is pressed up against the bathtub and my feet are near the door. My robe and gown are pushed up to my neck; my panties are wrapped around my right ankle. There's a black, thin, musty-smelling teenage boy on top of me—it's my brother, Andrew, humping up and down on me. Tears are running down the side of my face and I keep hollering, "Mama, Mama, help me!" There's a white rotary phone sitting on the toilet: it rings. Andrew picks it up and says, "Hello." I scream out, "Help me!" He covers my mouth and tells the person on the other end, "Mama is not here," then he hangs up the phone.

He gets up, pulls up his pants, and then tells me to get up. There's a terrible musty odor in the room. I pull up my panties and I notice that there is white thick slime running down my leg; that's where the odor is coming from. He lets me out of the bathroom to join my sister and nephews who are playing in the bedroom. I go to sit on the floor, but my privacy hurts as if something is still in it.

I awake now 30-years-old. I am lying in bed next to my fiancé. I am wearing green flannel pajamas and a red scarf on my head. Unable to fall back to sleep, I begin to watch TV. In two hours, it will be time to get up for work. I arrive at work where I serve as assistant director of an adult day program. As usual my day is busy; I have ten employees who I supervise to prevent neglect to mentally challenged clients. At the end of the day, I return back home to a ten-year-old son, two foster kids, and a fiancé.

Here I go again. It's 2:43 a.m. and I'm awakened. I begin to replay the dream in my mind. I'm five-years-old, in the back bedroom of an apartment, lying on a urine stained, blue and white stripped, twin size mattress. There are no sheets or blankets on the bed. I'm unable to see what I'm wearing and I don't see a face this time.

He's black and his chest is pressed up against my face. He's humping up and down on me and it feels as if he is ripping my privacy up. I'm trying to scream, but his chest is smothering my mouth. When he is done he lifts me up, pulls up my panties and sends me outside to play. This dream never allows me to see a face. On the way out the front door, I feel as if I'm peeing on myself. I look down and there's thick white slime running down my leg and a musty odor. I ask myself, "Why do I keep having these bad dreams?"

It's now 9:30 a.m., Saturday morning. I hear the kids moving around, so there's no sleeping in today. I will be serving the Saturday special: grits, eggs, bacon, and toast. Shortly after breakfast, the kids will dress and head out the door to play. I will do the usual weekend cleaning.

Finally, it's evening and time to take a break. I shower, put on my crème silk pajamas and pour myself a glass of chilled White Zinfandel. I sit on my black sunk in leather couch and begin to watch one of my favorite programs, *E.R.* Ten minutes into the show and the phone rings; it's Pam, my sister. That's it for *E.R.* When Pam and I get on the phone, it turns into a marathon. Pam is 31-years-old, married, and a mother of three. She is very dramatic, highly emotional, and suffers with suicidal thoughts. "Hey Pam, what's up?" She says that she is getting ready to check herself into John George Mental Institution. This is nothing unusual; this is a yearly occasion for her. I ask her, "What is it this time?" She begins to tell me how upset she is with our mother, for not protecting her when she was a kid. Our mother now acts as though what happened to her then can't possibly be affecting her now. I immediately go into agreement with her about our mother.

My mother, who is now in her 70's, is a retired school teacher and mother of nine kids. Very strong willed and intelligent; nothing ever gets pass her. But she tends to ignore things when it comes to her boys. She will commit a crime to protect them, and I never understood why. Pam and I are convinced that my mother was fully aware of the sexual abuse that happened to her. To confirm our feelings, we utilize three way calling and call a close family friend, Sheila. Sheila is older than Pam and I; she lives about two hours from us. She is a heavy drinker and chronic cigarette smoker, but honest. So Pam begins to question her about our upbringing. Then Pam gets specific and asks Sheila, if during the time that she was around us, did she ever hear anything about her getting molested. For about twenty seconds Sheila's end of the phone goes silent. Then Sheila tells us that she has been around our family since before we were born. Then she begins to tell us about one night in particular when she was visiting our house. She was in the bathroom preparing to go out with one of my older sisters when Pam knocked on the door and said she had to pee. Sheila opened the door and told her to come in and pee, while she continued to put on her makeup. As the urine began to flow, Pam started screaming. Sheila said, "What's wrong?" Pam said, "My pee pee hurt." Sheila said, "What happen to it?" Pam said, "Danny hurt it." Then Sheila said she noticed small spots of blood in Pam's panties. So Sheila said she called my older sister to the bathroom to take a look at Pam. The older sister came in and told Pam to get up and leave the bathroom, and she returned back to her room. Then Sheila begins to tell us about other situations and rumors about our family.

After about an hour of comical but disgusting conversation, Sheila says, "I never understood why mom never did anything to those no good boys, after all the stuff they did to ya'll." *Ya'll, who is ya'll?* I thought. *Ya'll, does ya'll mean Pam and I, or Pam and my other sisters? Who is ya'll?* I wouldn't dare ask. She couldn't be talking about me. I'm the assistant director of the day program, I drive a new car, I'm getting ready to get married, and my son is the best dressed at his school; she couldn't be including me.

Let me refill my glass, because now she got me tripping. Pam and I hang up with Sheila, and continue to talk for about another hour, and then we hang up. But my mind was still puzzled, *who is ya'll?* Then I began to wonder had I been having bad dreams or reliving bad memories. Why was the dream so clear, the smell so real, and the pain still felt? My mind is racing so fast in thoughts that it feels like it's about to explode. I pour myself another glass of wine in an attempt to calm my nerves. But my mind is still racing; I get so lost in thought that I eventually pass out to sleep.

Chapter 2

Growing Pains

I grew up in the Tassafaronga Projects, which was referred to as the 85th village. It was located on 85th Avenue in Oakland, CA. At the very tender age of five, I can vividly remember all the hurt and pain that we suffered as a family. My mom being a single parent of nine kids was truly overwhelmed. Not only was it ten of us, but one of my older sisters had three kids and one of them lived with us, while her other two kids stayed with their dad's mom. So we were all squeezed into a three bedroom apartment like sardines. It's sad but I can't recall not one happy moment in those projects. Living there was like living in hell. Well I guess I can't blame the place; I'd have to blame the people, especially the people in our house. It's said that our experiences shape us. So after reading this you may understand why I behave the way I do.

I grew up in a house with four brothers: Antonio, Derrick, Andrew, Danny, and four sisters: Yvonne and Yvette (who were twins), Pam, Denise and me, Andrea, but everyone called me T.C. I was the youngest of the nine. And being the youngest was no piece of cake. Either I was treated with favoritism for being the youngest, which created sibling jealousy or I was forgotten about. There was always bickering and fighting. If my brothers weren't fighting each other, they would be fighting with the neighborhood kids. We were often sent out in dirty clothes and shoes that had holes in them.

I can remember my mom going out to party with my two, oldest sisters and their friends. They were more like friends instead of mother and daughters. She would leave me and my six-year-old sister Pam home in the care of our teenage sister, Denise, who may have been sixteen at the time. Denise didn't prove to be a good baby sitter, because when my mom and the twins went out the front door, it wasn't long before Denise went out the back door heading to the recreation center in the projects where they held parties every weekend for teenagers. So Denise would put me and my sister to bed, leaving us unattended; and, she would go out with friends to party and then return home and hop into bed with us before my mom came home. And this went on for a while with my mom never knowing her secret. Then there were times when my mom didn't go out with her daughters; instead they gave a party at the house, partying to the wee hours of the morning. My sister Pam and I would pretend to be going to the bathroom to see what they were doing. Everyone would be standing around drinking and smoking cigarettes. A few people would be dancing. But the night never ended without someone fighting. The mornings after these parties, Pam and I would always get up early and discover Ripple and Thunderbird bottles on the floor that still contained alcohol. We would begin to play the records that they had left out. My favorite song was "Chain of Fools" by Aretha Franklin. I would hold an alcohol bottle to my mouth and pretend that it was a microphone and sing to the top of my lungs. Leading up to the awakening of my mother, who would then make us cut off the record player. We would then fix ourselves a bowl of cereal and sit in the middle of the floor among the cigarette ashes and empty bottles that were dropped from the night before.

Having a big family living in the projects wasn't unusual. It seemed like everyone in there had at least seven people living in their apartment, which didn't make it easy to have peace.

My oldest brother decided to go into the Navy, leaving the other three behind to continue on with their mischief. When they weren't fighting, they were breaking into the laundry mat, stealing all the coins, or breaking into trains as they stop at a nearby loading facility. At least once a week someone was knocking on our door complaining about my brothers. If it wasn't a neighbor, it was the police coming to arrest them. Then there were times when the welfare worker would come by and she was worse than the police. She would come by to inspect the house to see who all was living there. She would look in the closets, under the beds, and through the cabinets. When this happened, my mom would have me go over a couple of buildings to her best friend, Mary's house, whom we called Auntie Mary. See the social worker didn't know about me; my mom kept me a secret so that she would be able to get money and medical benefits from my dad and it not shorten her cash aid and food stamps. I was so much of a secret that my mom gave birth to me at home with the aid of my twin sisters and didn't take me to a doctor or to get a birth certificate until I was two-years-old.

    I would often go over to Auntie Mary's house to play with her kids, whom we referred to as our cousins. Auntie Mary also had nine kids. One day, while over there playing, I decided to take the dirt from the grass and build a castle underneath the stairs. My cousin, Mary's daughter Angie, was above me on the balcony playing with my nephew Kevin, my sister Yvonne's oldest boy, who was visiting for the day. They were on the balcony playing with old parts of a tricycle. Angie yelled down to me from the balcony and told me to get from under the stairs and to go in the house. Well with her being only a few years older than me, I didn't feel the need to have to obey her. So I continued to gather dirt and build my castle under the stairs. And they continued to play on the balcony above me. As I was carrying in a pale of dirt to complete my castle, Angie yelled out to me, "Watch out!" As I looked up to see what she was yelling for, something came down crashing into my head. It felt as if my whole head split open. The force of the object knocked me down to the pavement causing me to fall on my back. While on the ground, all I heard was Auntie Mary screaming and everything went black. When I came to, someone had me in their arms and was running me through the projects toward my house. By the time we reached our lawn, there must have been about 100 people out there, and as my mother came running to grab me, all I could hear was the sound of sirens. They laid me on the grass and everyone huddled over me. I must have blacked out again because the next thing I remembered was being on a gurney going through the emergency room doors and my father standing there waiting on us. By this time, my clothes and the gurney were soaked with blood. Someone on that balcony had dropped the handle bars of the tricycle on my head, above my right eye. There was so much blood in my eye that the doctors thought that my eye ball had been knocked out. But after a few hours in the hospital, the doctor came out and told my parents that my eye was fine, but that the handle bars had cracked my skull. They had to shave the right side of my head so that they could clean the area and stitch it up, and after a few days, it would be okay to take me home. While at the hospital, I heard that my Auntie Mary put a whooping on her daughter, Angie that could be heard throughout the whole projects.

    I was soon released to go home, where my mom would have to change my bandage daily until the wound healed. I can still remember the bad headaches associated with the wound, and my mom giving me some pink Bayer aspirin for kids to help with the pain. I wasn't allowed to go outside for weeks.

    Soon after my recovery, my two twin sisters moved out into their places. Also two of my brothers had finally gotten caught for stealing and were in juvenile hall. So my mom decided, after landing a teacher's assistance job, we were moving out of the projects and into a much better neighborhood. So we packed up and moved into a two bedroom apartment. My mom, I and my two other sisters would share a room, and the youngest teenage boy would occupy the other room alone.

    Well mom was right about one thing, this neighborhood is much better than the projects. With the older siblings being gone, we don't have as much company, making it easier to spend more time with mom. She would get us up early every Saturday to clean up before *Soul Train* came on. *Soul Train* was a live recording of dancing and performances by various singers and groups. Watching *Soul Train*, you would get to see all the latest fashions and learn all the new dances. *Soul Train* was called the hippest trip in town. Once *Soul Train* went off, my mom, Pam and I would pile into my mom's station wagon and head to my dad's house. Although my mom had nine kids and five baby daddies, my dad was the only one we saw on a regular basis. Elijah Henry, who stood about 6'1", and weighed about 200 pounds, was 50-years-old when my mom gave birth to me. He had served in the United States Navy since he was an adult. After the Navy, he got a job at an oil company. He was well known and liked in the area where he lived—especially with the ladies. My dad had about five girlfriends, but that didn't include my mom. Their relationship was over; they just remained good friends. My mom knew about his girlfriends and never seemed bothered when he would talk about them or take Pam and me to visit them. Because Pam and I were so close in age, my mom had one rule that she strongly enforced. And that was: if you do for one girl you had to do for the other, which even as a child I thought was stupid. I will never forget the day my dad showed up to our house with a bag full of new clothes for me that one of his girlfriends had purchased. I remember opening the bag and finding some red pattern leather clogs, and a two piece blue jean suit with a matching hat. I immediately put on the shoes and began parading around the house. My mom became furious and made me put everything back in the bag and told my dad that I couldn't have it, because there was nothing for Pam. My dad picked up the bag and left. I ran into my room and cried for what seemed liked forever. My dad lived about 20 minutes from us in an area that was referred to as West Oakland. He lived between two of the meanest streets in town, Market and San Pablo. On San Pablo, you could find all the prostitutes and pimps, and on Market you could find all the heroine dealers and users. I was fascinated every time I went to my dad's because there was so much action. Prostitutes would be out there in swim suits and rabbit coats; pimps would be pulling up in Cadillac's and Limousines. People would be using dope right out in the open. And you were guaranteed to see a fight every weekend. My sister Pam and I would sit in the yard on my dad's car all day and just watch the people roam up and down the street. So much so, that we knew them by name. We even dreaded going home on Sunday night.

It didn't take us long to get to know the people in our four unit apartment building. As a matter of fact, my mother befriended the lady upstairs from us, making her our new babysitter. She had two daughters named Tony and Donna who attended the same school as Pam and me, which was also the same school where my mom worked as a teacher's assistant. Pam and I are now in the first and second grade. My mom would send us upstairs when she left for work, which was an hour difference before our school bell rang. So we would walk with Tony and Donna who were in the fourth and fifth grade. Tony and Donna were not that easy on the eye and they both dressed like boys. Although they would be nice to Pam, Donna, the younger sister, was always mean to me. Every since my mom had landed the new job and was collecting money from my dad weekly, Pam and I always had nice clothes with matching hair accessories. Everyone would always tell me how cute I was and always asked me to sing which angered Donna greatly. She would always pick on me, telling me that I was ugly and nobody liked me. One morning while walking to school in my new red turtle neck sweater and my red and blue plaid pleated skirt, Donna walked up behind me and kicked up my skirt, exposing my underwear to a crowd of people behind us. Everyone laughed at me and teased me for days. Even as a child I knew that she was just mad because she was ugly. Her mom even showed me favoritism when I would be at their house after school waiting on my mom to come get us. She loved to comb my long, black, thick hair and decorate it with ribbons and barrettes. Donna and Tony both had short, nappy hair. The times that we would have to stay at their house, Donna was repeatedly mean to me. I remember one time she even trying to make me eat some dirt from the yard. I hated being with them, but for some reason I never told my mom about how Donna treated me.

My middle sister, Denise, had a boyfriend who had his own place, so she was very seldom at the house. My mom continued to hang out with my twin sisters, but not at the clubs. Both twins were now married and had families. Yvonne had four kids and Yvette had one. They all developed a love for roller derby skating matches and shopping. So they would go out several days a week leaving my teenage brother to baby sit us in the evenings and on some Saturdays. Normally, when the parent is away kids would pull together as a team and get into mischief. But such was not the case.

    I mean there was a time when we baked a cake without any eggs, and the cake came out like a rubber ball. So we had fun tossing it all around the house. But then there was a time when I was brutally raped. I remember this incident as if it were yesterday. My mom and the twins were out shopping, leaving Pam and I and Yvonne's two oldest boys home alone with my brother. He told us all to go into his room and lay on the floor to take a nap. Then he told me to come here and took me into a small bathroom. He laid me there on the bathroom floor, on top of a pink carpet, and pulled my underwear down to my ankle, with my top pulled up, and his musty body on top of me, humping up and down with his penis inside of me feeling like its ripping my body apart. I'm crying; but, his chest is smothering my mouth. And my head is constantly hitting up against the tub. Then the phone rings. So he lifts his chest off of my face. There's a white rotary phone sitting on the toilet. He grabs the phone and I hear my mom's brother on the other end asking for her. I scream out, "Help!" He covers my mouth, and tells my uncle that my mom is gone and hangs up the phone. He then tells me to get up and pull up my clothes. Then he sends me out crying into the room with the other kids who are looking at me strange when I enter the room. As I go to sit on the floor my privacy hurts so bad that I scream out in pain. No one in the room said a word to me, and my brother never even turned around to see what had happened. Then there's another incident when my mother is gone, and Pam and I are left with him. Someone knocks on the door and he puts Pam and I in the hall closet and tells us to shut up. He answers the door and my sister Yvonne comes in asking for mom. He tells her that mom is gone. Yvonne then says, "Where are the girls?" Upon hearing Yvonne's voice, I bust out of the closet and run to her. She looks at him very sternly and then tells Pam and me to get our coats and come with her. Later that evening my mom comes to pick us up from Yvonne. But there is no discussion about us being in the closet. As terrified as I was when I ran out, there is no way that Yvonne could have thought that we were playing a game. I remember a time being in the backyard sitting in the dirt and crying, and the teenage boys who lived next door to us came and asked me what was wrong. I told them what my brother had done to me; and, they questioned me about the size and the color of his penis; then, they all walked away laughing at my story. I sat there in the dirt crying and covered my face with my sweater. Even as a child, I felt embarrassed.

Other than these horrible events, things in our house went on as usual—school for us and work for my mom.

The regular school year is ending and my sister Pam and I will be spending the summer at my dad's house. And I can't wait to get away from the babysitter's daughter, Donna. My mom has already said that next school year Pam and I will be old enough to leave from home by ourselves and walk to school.

During the summer break, the government has established a first time home buyer program. My mom, who has been faithfully attending the workshops, finds out that she qualifies to get a house with no money down, and has informed us, that within a few months we would be moving into our own home. After searching for weeks, mom finally finds a home that she likes. Although it's only about 10 minutes from where we are now, it's an all-residential neighborhood. The house is all white, two stories and has a huge back yard with an apple and a lemon tree and it sits on the corner of 92nd and Peach Street. We immediately begin to pack. Well moving day has finally arrived. Family comes over and helps us get settled in. Although the house is large, it only has two bedrooms upstairs and an oversized room downstairs. So my mom puts my older sister Denise, Pam and myself in the front bedroom and she takes the back room, leaving the downstairs open for my brothers. Two were in the Army and the oldest one had been released from the Navy and had moved to Los Angeles, CA. The other one was in jail for petty theft.

The first night in the house was magical. It felt so peaceful being in a room big enough for three beds. We even had a TV in the room. My sister Denise was older now and was able to come in late or stay out all night, leaving Pam and I the freedom to lay in the dark and talk for what seemed like hours until one of us fell asleep. The next day, Pam and I got dressed and headed outside to explore the neighborhood. We met a boy about 10 years-old named Michael. Michael told us that our house was haunted and that someone was killed in the basement. Being kids we didn't think much of his comment, so we continued on down the street to meet up with another group of kids who were playing tetherball. We introduced ourselves and were invited to play with them. When we got back home I called my dad, told him about the kids, and that they owned a tetherball. He said that he would buy us one and bring it by on the weekend. Saturday morning came and with it came my daddy, with a long string in his hand with a bright yellow ball attached to it. Pam and I jumped for joy and immediately ran outside to climb up the corner street sign to attach our tetherball. By the time the other kids came outside, Pam and I were already playing. And within minutes everyone was standing in front of our house waiting for their turn to play. That day we met almost every kid within a three block radius. Every day and every weekend that the weather permitted and we weren't at my dad's, we were outside playing tetherball. Everything seems to finally be going good. My mom is happy with her job and the friends that she has made. Denise has a boyfriend and is expecting a baby. Pam and I have new friends and one of my brothers will be coming home from jail soon.

Stonehurst Elementary School, September of 1977. Pam has been placed in a gifted class for extremely smart students and my mom is one of her instructors. I have joined the music class. I love to sing and my teacher thinks that I have a wonderful voice. Not only does she work with me alone after school, she has also booked me to sing at a fashion show and a beauty pageant. She is also preparing me to do a musical with a choir called, "It's Music", which we will travel from school to school doing. And she has given me all the lead parts. She always tells me that I have a lovely voice and to keep on singing. I don't think that I have good voice; I just know that I love to sing, plus no one in my family ever tells me that I sound good to them. With me traveling with the choir and Pam being in so many projects, the school year flies by. And it's now summer again. Mom informs us that we will not be going to our dad's house this summer but that we will stay at our house and just visit with him. This is cool because we have so many new friends here that we rarely get to see, because we don't attend the neighborhood school; we go to school in another district.

My mom has just received a call from my brother Antonio saying that he was being released from jail. Upon his release he soon meets a 16-year-old girl. Shortly after dating, she gets pregnant. Although my brother is three years older than she is, her family still allows him to see her. They have a baby girl, but soon after the baby is born they split up. The girl decided that she wanted to date other people and my brother was not happy with that.

One day while my mom, Pam and I are sitting on the living room floor watching TV, there's a knock on the door. When my mom opens the door and sees two police officers, she is not surprised; her boys were always getting into trouble. So she has an expression of "what is it now". The officer tells her to have Pam and I leave the room. While the other officer asks for permission to search Antonio's room, my mom sends Pam and me into our bedroom which is located right next to the living room. So I sit on the floor with the door cracked, with my cheek pressed on the door allowing me to see my mother's face. The officer begins to question her about my brother, Antonio's whereabouts a few nights ago; then, he begins to whisper to my mom. My mom's eyes become bucked and she places her hand over her mouth in an attempt to smother the scream that is about to come out. She removes her glasses as tears roll down her cheeks, and she holds her head tightly with both hands as if it is going to explode. As I sit there, an 11-year-old girl with my face pressed up against the door, I begin to cry silently for my mother. Pam sits next to me with her head held down not knowing what is going on. She looked up and saw my tears but never said a word. When the police left, my mom got on the phone and called my older twin sister and asked her to come to the house immediately. She arrived within minutes. Then I overheard my mom say that Antonio was in jail, and then her voice begins to crack making it impossible for me to understand her. My older sister came into our room and told Pam and I to pack some clothes because we were all going to my dad's house. She dropped us three off at my dad's and then phoned Denise and told her to stay where she was at. When my dad came in from work, my mom took him in the bedroom to talk. By the time they came out of the room, my mom's whole body was shaking. She was so shook up that she was smoking cigarette after cigarette. She just kept shaking her head, saying, "No, No." So my dad told Pam and I to go into our room so that my mom could rest. Pam and I sat in the bedroom not saying a word to each other. We just sat on the bed until my dad called us out to eat, and then told us to go to bed afterwards. While lying in bed, we turned on the TV and there was a reporter, Van Amburg discussing a phone call that he had received earlier that day from a man which led to the body: a 16-year-old girl who had been murdered. They showed my brother Antonio in the back of the police car and showed the duplex where they found her body. Now I know why my mom was shaking and crying. When Antonio's baby mama told him that she no longer wanted to see him, he became so frustrated that one night he set outside her home behind a tree and waited for her to return home. When she returned home, a man dropped her off. My brother approached her and talked her into going into a nearby vacant duplex to talk with him. During the discussion things became heated, she begins to scream, and he grabs her by the neck and begins choking her in an attempt to make her be quiet. Within minutes her body goes limp, and she is not breathing. He panics and runs out leaving her in the duplex alone. The next day he goes back and she is still lying on the floor breathless. He then calls a friend and has him go take a look at her, and the friend tells him that she is dead. Antonio then becomes fearful of what the police might do to him. So he phones the local news channel and asks for the lead reporter, Van Amburg and tells him to meet him at the duplex where he thinks he has killed his girlfriend.

The reporter arrives and finds the girl's body and immediately calls the police. He then tells Antonio to stay near him until they arrive and promises him that he won't let them beat him up. Police arrives, finds the girl and takes Antonio into custody. The police go two houses over and tell the girl's family that they have found her dead. After hearing the words of the reporter, I buried my face in the pillow and began to cry. Pam and I still don't say a word to each other. The next morning when I got up to go to the restroom, I overheard my dad say to my mom that he thinks it's best that we all stay with him for a while, just in case the girl's family tries to retaliate on us for what my brother had done. I peeped in at my mom and she never opened her mouth; she just shook her head 'yes'. Days has gone by now and my mom is still shaking and smoking cigarettes. She hasn't said a word to Pam and me since we left home. And my dad just tells us to leave her alone; she needs to rest. In the past when we would come to my dad's house, we would have fun; but, this trip was different. Pam and I are not allowed to go outside. And my dad won't let us watch TV. So we just sit in the washroom looking at old photos while playing his record player. My dad finally talks my mom into going to the doctor and after a few minutes in his office, the doctor tells my dad that my mom has suffered a nervous breakdown and that it will be a while before she can return back to work. We stayed at my dad's for two months, the whole duration of the summer. But school was getting ready to start again, and my mom refused to let us transfer, so she told my dad that it was time for us to go back home. When we got home, we weren't allowed to go outside, so we didn't get to see our friends. By me going to school in another district, I didn't have to deal with the embarrassment of everyone knowing what my brother had done. Although the teachers knew and was very concerned about my mother, they never questioned us in front of the other kids. They would keep us after the bell rang to be dismissed and then ask how our mother was doing. We would both say, "She fine", remembering that my mom had said earlier, "Whatever happens in this house stays in this house."

Growing Pains

    Two weeks after being back home and into school, someone set our front porch on fire. Fire fighters arrived in enough time to put it out, causing minimal damage. My twin sisters came by in an attempt to rescue us, but by mom refused to leave. I don't know if she was being courageous or if it was the medicine that she was on. Pam and I went into a survivor's mode. We would go to school, come home, do homework and fix our own food, while my mom would lie on the couch, smoking Pall Mall Red cigarettes, drinking orange soda, and taking valiums all day. My dad would come out on the weekends and take us all to his house, to wash clothes and then drop us back home on Sunday evenings. After months of court hearings, my brother was sentenced, but it was never said to us how long he would be in jail. Then one day my mom finally got up. She told Pam and me that we all would be going to L.A. to see my oldest brother and his family for the summer. This was perfect timing because our home had become infested with fleas due to the death of our dog, Fritzie. We packed our bags and boarded the Greyhound bus headed for Los Angeles. This would be Pam's and my first visit to L.A. so we were excited. We had seen many pictures and heard lots of stories about Disneyland. Upon getting to my brother's house, we learned that he, his wife, and his son were all Muslims which meant no bacon, no dry salami, and no pork chops. He had very strict rules about what we could do and where we could go. We were only allowed to play in the front yard of his small home. His house had only two bedrooms which put my mom, Pam and I all in a full size bed. Can you imagine how uncomfortable that was? At 11 o'clock at night, it's still 75 degrees outside, and here we are, all three of us cramped up in a little bed with me in the middle. Not only was it hot and sweaty, but I would spend all night itching from flea bites. My legs, back and arms were covered with blisters and open sore from all of the scratching. I would spend most of the night tossing, turning, and scratching. I hate having to sleep in the bed in this hot house with them. I hate being here; I wish I could go to my dad's house like we do every summer. Plus all we do is sit on the porch, watch TV and listen to the radio, while my mom spends all her time in the garage sewing. One day, I went into the garage to complain to my mom about how boring it is here and ask her if we could go to Disneyland. She tells me that we are not here to go to Disneyland; we are here to visit family. So I go into our room and sit on the bed with my lips poked out. My brother comes in to tell me that he is taking us all to a convention with him to see "the Honorable Elijah Muhammad", who is the leader of the Muslims on Saturday, which is in two days.

When Saturday arrives, my mom gets Pam and me up to bathe and get dressed. She dresses us up in white slacks and pink silk shirts with a bow, curls our hair and tells us to be quiet when we get there and don't ask for nothing. We arrive at a huge stadium and there are thousands of women with scarves on their heads and all the men are wearing bow ties and are very polite. We take our seats in the balcony with my brother's wife, who is about 5'5", 135 pounds with very pretty, brown, flawless skin and some big, brown eyes. Even though I don't like being here, she is always very nice to us. After about 30 minutes into the program, they finally bring out Elijah Muhammad, and among the men escorting him to the podium is my brother. When I see him I look over at mom; she is sitting there with tears in her eyes, but not sorrowful tears; I think in some way she is proud of him. Elijah Muhammad must have spoke for about two hours straight, and my brother stood by his side the entire time like a robot. And Pam and I sat there quietly the entire time. But I still never understood what he was talking about. However, everyone else must have understood because they stood and clapped when he was done. As we begin to drive back to my brother's house, I was wishing we were driving back to Oakland. I want to go home!

Chapter 3

So You Think You're A Woman

It is my first day at Elmhurst Junior High School. I am so excited to be home from L.A., to see all my friends, and attend a new school that I could hardly sleep last night. My mom had spent the whole summer in L.A. sewing our school clothes which was much cheaper than buying them. So Pam and I had over 10 outfits each. By now, I have started combing my own hair, which is very manageable—thanks to the perm that my mom allowed us to get. I'm in the seventh grade standing about 5', long, black hair, and measurements are 33-25-34. Oh yeah, I am a young woman now. Boys are all over me due to my cute shape and these tailored made clothes are the icing on the cake. I have so many friends that it's crazy. I have friends from my elementary school, friends from my neighborhood, and new friends that I have just met. Pam got here a year before me, so she has already established a reputation for herself as the best dresser and a honor roll student. So she spends all her time with the smarty pants. Me? I'm a little more sociable. I hang with the "in crowd": The well known girls and the coolest guys. And although I'm younger than a lot of them, my grown attitude allows me to fit in. It took me a few weeks to get used to having to switch classes every hour, but I'm finally getting the hang of it. My American Government teacher, Mr. Williams, is super cool. He is also over all the student activities. One day he pulls me aside in the hallway and tells me that

I should consider running for seventh grade class president, or a position on the student body. He says that I have strong leadership qualities and believes that I could win. So I agree to run and immediately begin to spend my lunch breaks in the library making "vote for me" signs.

So I began to make a name for myself at Elmhurst Junior High School as a class president, cheerleader and honor roll student. But not only was I making a name for myself academically and in school politics, but also with the "in crowd". I had an entourage of girls who I hung out with and a lot of guys wanted to date me. I remember one guy in particular on the basketball team who liked me, but I thought he was ugly. I told someone that he looked like a frog and they told him. So that day on my way home from school, he ran up behind me to confront me about what I said and he slapped me in my face. I went home and told my mom and the next morning she came up to the school and had him suspended. Although there was only a few people who actually witnessed the incident, the word had spread around the school quickly about what had happened. So all day everyone is looking at me to see if my face is bruised. I just continue to go to class and act as if nothing is wrong while hiding the embarrassment and hurt in my heart. A few days later when the boy returned to school, he apologized to me and told me that he really liked me and wanted me to be his girlfriend. So we became boyfriend and girlfriend. He was one-year older than me. But the relationship didn't last long because there were too many other guys who I wanted to hang out with. I must admit, at first I was little frightened of junior high school but now I'm really enjoying it; it is so much fun. I don't hang with a lot of girls my age except for my best friend. My best friend's name is Brenda who lives around the corner from us. Brenda and I are about the same height and measurements. We often wear each other's clothes. Brenda and I walk to and from school together every day. We are inseparable. We do everything together, from school to hanging out every day, going out to parties and clubs on the weekends, to going to church on Sundays. One day during lunch break, Brenda and I joined a group of ninth graders on the field who were smoking weed (marijuana). They passed the weed to Brenda and me and we hit it a few times. A few minutes later, when the bell rang to return to class, I got up from the grass, and became immediately dizzy. When I tried to take a step, it felt as if I was walking in clouds and my legs were stuck. I used my hands to try to lift my legs. Everyone on the field was laughing at me as I walked passed them. Somehow I made it to my typing class. But my teacher noticed that something was wrong and she had me escorted to the office. And although I was aware of my surroundings, I didn't know what was going on with me. It was like I was outside of myself watching myself. Once in the office, they told me to lay my head on the table for a while and wait for the vice principal. About 10 minutes later, the vice principal walks in with the dean and they begin to question me about what I had been doing all morning. They then inform me that the school patrol saw me sitting with a group of kids during lunch who are known for smoking weed. So I admitted that I had smoked some weed with them that they had bought from another student on campus. By the time they were through questioning me, they had the names of six other students who were smoking weed and the dealer, and I was being suspended for three days. This was fine by me because I was experiencing some strange things. When I got home from school my mom didn't even fuss at me; I think she was too concerned about how the weed had affected me. I kept having dizzy spells and from time to time my eyes would get really big and then close, causing me to forget momentarily where I was. When I returned back to school I found out that what I had smoked was some Marijuana laced with PCP, a chemical that causes you to hallucinate and become very violent when used in excess.

Well ya'll time is flying by. Pam has graduated and went on to high school, which puts me in the ninth grade, and my last year of junior high school. I am now the head cheerleader, class and student body president, so I am always getting pulled out of class for different meetings. In between class, work, and school politics, Brenda and I often perform in the school talent shows. We have a dance group called the "Supagroovalistics", with Brenda, me, and a guy from the neighborhood. We have won first place in the talent shows twice. But for the upcoming talent show, I have decided to do something other than dance. I have decided to sing. Yep, sing! I haven't done any singing since I left elementary school. The talent show went well; although, I didn't win, quite a few people came up to me and told me that I had a nice voice and that I should consider joining the choir when I get to high school.

Brenda and I have both turned 14 years old and have outgrown the boys here at our school. So we moved on to dating high school boys. One day on the way home from a school dance, Brenda and I met two boys who were at the park playing basketball. They told us that they were sophomores in high school and we exchanged phone numbers with them. So almost every day after school, Brenda and I would go to their neighborhood and hang out with them. I was no longer yearning to go to my dad's on the weekend. I had gotten too old for that. I wanted to stay home and go clubbing with Pam and her friends. That's right—clubbing. There was a club located in San Francisco, called the Palladium for 18 and older. Well at least that's what the sign said, but they never asked for any I.D. So when Pam would hop in the car with one of the older girls in the neighborhood whom she had become very close friends with, Brenda and I would hop in with her. None of us was 18, but that didn't stop us from going. This had become our regular routine. We would arrive there at about 9:00 p.m. and wouldn't leave until it closed at 4:00 am. Sometimes when we pulled up to our house, it would be daylight and my mom never stopped us from going or said anything about the time that we got in. I had become as comfortable with coming and going as I pleased that I had even started hanging out on school nights, not getting home until after 11:00 p.m. The whole time my mom never said a word. I don't know if she just didn't care or she was so worn out from the other eight kids that she just didn't have the strength to discipline me. Whatever the reason was, it was fine by me. I was going out and partying every time I heard that something was going on. I would just tell her that I was going with the neighborhood kids and that we would all stick together. She never once tried to confirm my story; she just went with the flow. Before long, I was grown and wild. By the time I got into the 10th grade, my body was fully developed. I was what you called a "brick house". When I would be walking to school, men would pull over and try to talk to me, telling me how pretty I was and what a great shape I had. But I never fail for those lines. I had hooked back up with an old boyfriend from junior high school. "The frog", the boy who had slapped me for saying he looked like a frog. He was still playing basketball and I had become a cheerleader. We would often skip school and go to his house while his mom was away at work. Doing this on a regular basis could only lead to one thing: sex. We would lie up in his bed like two grown folk. We would lie there for hours listening to Luther Vandross until it was time for school to end; then he would walk me home. We got so comfortable in our relationship that I stopped going to the clubs on Saturdays and started spending the night over his house. He would sneak me in through the window when his mom went to sleep and I would leave before she awakened in the morning.

One Monday morning, as I got up for school, my stomach became very sick. "I must be catching the flu." So I decided to eat some crackers and drink some juice. I managed to get dressed and make it to school. But before I could make it to my classroom door, I threw up right there in the hallway. The hall patrol lady came and took me to the nurse. The nurse allowed me to lie in her office until I felt better and then sent me to my next class. The next day I woke up feeling the same way. So what I decided to do was drink some juice and hang around the house for a while just in case I needed to throw up. Glad I followed my first mind because as soon as the juice went down, it came right back up. So this became my routine for about two weeks: get up, drink juice, and vomit. So in the mornings before school I'm vomiting; when I get out of school, I come home and go right to sleep. I had been spending so much time laying up and being grown that I had not noticed that my period hadn't arrived for two months. My boyfriend kept asking me what was wrong with me and telling me to go to the doctor. But I couldn't go to the doctor without my mother finding out. She had my medical card. So one day while at school I asked one of the older girls on the cheering squad if she knew of a doctor that I could go to for free. She told me to go to the health clinic which was right next door to our high school. So on the way home, I stopped by and told the triage nurse how I had been feeling. She gave me a number and told me to take a seat. About a half an hour later my number was called. I went into the office and told the nurse practitioner my symptoms and she told me to pee in a cup. She took the cup and poured the urine on a stick and within seconds she told me that I was pregnant. According to my last menstrual period, I was two months. I told her that I wanted to have an abortion. She asked me did I have any medical insurance and I lied and said no. She gave me the address of the county welfare office where I could go and receive a free medical card without my parents knowing that could only be used for the abortion. The next day I skipped school and went straight to the welfare office. I was there all day filling out papers that a 15-year-old my age didn't even understand. I just wrote down what I thought they wanted to hear, and that was that we were poor, had no job, no money, and no bank accounts. Then I turned them in. They told me to return the next day to find out their decision. I hopped on the bus and went home as if I had been in school all day. I went straight into my room to lie down and take a nap. Later that evening, my boyfriend called to check on me and to find out why I wasn't at school. I told him where I had gone and that I had to return tomorrow. With him being only 16-years-old, he didn't know what to say; so, he said, "Okay. I will call you tomorrow." The next morning I got up and made my way back to the welfare office to be there at 9:00 a.m. when they opened. When I got there, there was already about 25 people ahead of me. By the time they got to me, it was after lunch and all the smells of food had me so nauseated that I thought I was going to pass out. By the time the worker got half way through my paper work, I had laid my head on the table. The worker looked up at me and told me to come back next Tuesday which was six days away to come pick up my medical card. I left there in enough time to make it to school before

So You Think You're A Woman

the last bell rang. I went into the gym to tell the cheerleader instructor that I had not been feeling well and that I would get a note from my mom to bring her. On the way out the gym, I ran into my boyfriend. He asked me how was I feeling and I said, "Not too good." He touched my stomach and asked what the welfare people said. I told him I had to go back next week to get the card for the abortion. I then told him I had to hurry home because I wasn't feeling well. He said okay, and that he would call me later. For the next two days at school, I kept to myself. I would go to class and then sit alone at lunch time on the stairs in the hallway. I would sit there and rub my stomach while eating an orange, and pretend that I was keeping the baby. Those two days seemed like the loneliest time of my life. It was like although everybody saw me, no one noticed that something was wrong. None of my friends even asked where had I been, or why was I sick every day? My boyfriend and I hadn't even been spending a lot of time together; he was still playing basketball and hanging out with his friends, while I was trying to figure out how to handle this without anyone finding out about it. Tuesday finally arrived and I skipped school again to go and get the medical card. When they gave me the medical card, they also gave me a list of numbers to gynecologists in my area that accepted the medical card. When I got home I immediately began calling numbers and lucked up and found a doctor within 15 minutes and walking distance from my home. They even told me I could come in the next morning for an appointment. So again I missed another day of school. The doctor called me to the back and explained the whole procedure to me and said that he could perform the procedure the following morning at 9:00 a.m. I made the appointment and went home to get some rest. I was so weak from vomiting every morning and worrying about how this was going to turn out that I was drained. When my mom came in from work, I was sleep. She woke me up and sat on the edge of my bed and questioned me about why I had not been eating and about the swelling of my breast. I told her that I was pregnant and that I had gotten a medical card and that the abortion was to take place the next morning. She asked me how was I getting there and who was going with me? I told her I was catching the bus by myself. She said that she would take off work and take me; then she walked out of the room. The next morning my mom drove me to the doctor. They were ready for me as soon as I walked in the door. The nurse took me to the back and had me undress. Then she asked if I wanted my mom to come in with me. I told the nurse no; due to my embarrassment, I didn't want my mom with me. They offered me a valium to help keep me calm, but I refused. When I lay back on the table, I noticed next to the bed a glass machine with a vacuum hose attached to it. The doctor comes in and tells me that the procedure will hurt but that it won't take long. He places my feet in the stirrups and then inserts the end of the hose inside of me. And then I hear the machine come on. As the machine comes on I immediately feel excruciating pain in my lower abdomen. It feels as if the machine is ripping my inside out. I'm crying out in pain and the nurse is there holding my hand and wiping my tears telling me that it will soon be over. Finally the machine cuts off and the nurse steps away from me to help the doctor. I look over at the machine and the glass container is now filled with blood and something that looks like raw meat. And then it dawns on me that it must be the baby. They take me into another room with a small bed and tell me to rest a minute before going home. After about 30 minutes, I realized that the pain wasn't going to get any better, so I got up and asked to go home. When I walked into the waiting room, bent over in pain, everyone in there looked up at me. One lady turned to her friend and whispered in her ear, and they both shook their heads in disgust. The receptionist told me that my mom had gone to the car to wait for me. When I reached the car my mom was sitting in the driver's seat with her glasses slumped down on her nose reading a book. I got into the car and neither one of us said a word.

When we reached home, my mom told me when she came into the room, with soup for me in hand, that she heard me crying from the waiting room of the Dr's Office. And immediately it registered to me. That's why everyone looked at me when I walked into the waiting area. That explains the whispering and the shaking of the heads. Later on that day, my mom walks into my room and says that she hopes that I never put myself in that predicament again. I just looked up at her and lay back down in pain. I don't know how long the procedure lasted, but I know the pain lasted all day. The next morning I was still very sore and experiencing cramps; so, I decided to stay home from school. With all this missing of school my grades had dropped extremely low. When I did return back to school, my cheerleading instructor asked me if I was pregnant, and that she had noticed the changes in my body. I told her no, that my dad had passed and that I had not been doing well. I think she knew that I was lying, but she didn't call me on it.

My junior year in high school flew by. My best friend and I were back hanging out on a regular. We made every house party there was on the weekends. Our lives consisted of school, boys, and partying. By the time we became seniors, she was pregnant and expecting a baby, and I was living with my new grown boyfriend. I had moved out of my mom's house and had begun living at his house. He would drop me off at school on his way to work. I felt so grown that I really had no interest in school. The only exciting thing about it was that I was a part of the Castleers' choir. We traveled from state to state singing and winning competitions. I still had a nice voice and a strong desire to sing. But I was just too caught up in being grown to stay committed to practicing with the group. So before the end of the school year, I quit the choir. I didn't attend any senior events, besides the senior ball and I just went there to take pictures. All this school stuff just seemed too juvenile for me. I just wanted it to be over. I lived with my boyfriend for about a year before it came to a bitter end. One Sunday, while visiting his mom, we got into an argument about something stupid. As he attempted to walk out the door, I jumped in front of him to prevent him from leaving. He pushed me out of the way causing me to fall. When I fell I heard something crack. When I looked to see what it was, I saw my left foot bent under my leg. When I tried to stretch it out, it wouldn't move. So I used my hand to pull it from under my leg. When I finally got it out, pain shot up my leg to my thigh. I screamed out in pain. By this time my ankle had swollen up so much that we had to cut my tennis shoe off. I immediately told him to give me the phone so I could call my sister, Denise. My sister came and got me and rushed me to the hospital. The doctor came in, ordered some x-rays and gave me something for the pain. Within minutes, he returned to tell me that I was being admitted into the hospital. My ankle had been broken on both sides and the bones were completely crushed. They put my foot in a temporary cast and sedated me before taking me up to my room.

The next day my boyfriend came up to the hospital to explain to my parents about what had happened. While he was explaining, three doctors walked in and told me that I would have to have surgery; they needed to remove the crushed bones and place a medal plate on both sides of my ankle and five screws to hold the plates in place to connect my foot to my leg. My mom almost passed out just from hearing the news. My boyfriend dropped his head in shame and my dad and I just looked at each other, but never said a word. I stayed in the hospital for about two weeks before they let me go home. When they released me, I went back to my boyfriend's house. But by now the relationship was over; we couldn't even fake like it was going to work. So he gathered my things as I held onto my crushes and I moved back to my mom's house.

Within a month, I had hooked up with some girls from the neighborhood and was back being an 18-year-old. Although I was still on crutches, that didn't stop me from hanging out. When I found out that my ankle would never be the same that I would walk with a limp and that I would never be able to wear high heeled shoes, I decided to get me a lawyer and sue my boyfriend for his actions. The lawyer said I wouldn't get much because the hospital would take most of it because my medical insurance expired when I turned 18, but that I would get something. When you're 18 and broke, something is better than nothing.

Chapter 4

Baby Mama Drama

Late one night in February while at a burger stand with friends, I met a guy by the name of Rod. He was a tall, dark, handsome guy with big, brown eyes. He was 19 and I was 18. We exchanged beeper numbers and began to hook up regularly. I would often go to a drug infested neighborhood where Rod sold drugs and hang out with him. We would hang out until about 2:00 a.m. on the drug turf, and then go and rent a motel for the night. That was the basis of our relationship. One morning, about a month into our relationship, I woke up feeling nauseated. I got dressed and went to McDonalds for a cheeseburger. A few bites into the burger and I had to throw up. I knew this feeling. *But I can't be pregnant, my stomach is cramping right now, my period is going to start any minute. I'm probably catching the flu. I'll just go back home and lay down for a while.*

   I awoke at the sound of my mom coming in the door from work. *Wow, its 6:00 p.m. already. Oh well I'm feeling better, guess I will call my road dog Lisa and hang out for a while.* Lisa was the only friend that I had who had a car. She was also well known in the neighborhood for her good looks and good girl reputation. Whenever Lisa and I get together, we usually ride through all of the drug turfs to see who's hanging out only to end up sitting on the hood of her car eating Chinese food and talking with Rod and his friends.

   Well its Saturday ya'll—my favorite day of the week. Why? Because, it's party time. Everybody who is somebody will be

Who Cried For The Little Girl

hanging out at the Lucky Lion Nightclub. Although I am still feeling a little sick, I'm still clubbing tonight! If this feeling isn't gone by Monday, I will go to the health clinic. Alright it's 10:00 p.m. and time to hit the club. I got on my tight jeans, got my hair did, and I'm feeling like a million bucks. Rod is here with all his friends and he's checking me out as I walk by. The club is jumping, people are everywhere, and everyone is in a good mood. Especially me, because I know when the club is over, Rod and I will go and get a room and call it a night.

Ok it's Monday, and as promised, I am on my way to the clinic. My stomach still feels nauseated. I don't know what could be wrong with me; this feeling reminds me of when I was pregnant, but even as I sit here, my stomach is cramping. Finally after sitting here for 30 minutes, they call me in to pee in a cup. Within seconds the nurse practitioner looks at me with no remorse and tells me that I am pregnant and gives me a due date of December 25, 1985. *What!! But my stomach is cramping; my period is going to start. Oh my God! Lord what am I going to do? I don't have a job; I don't even have medical insurance. This is crazy! What am I going to do?*

After hearing the news, I begin to walk home. What should have been a 10 minute walk seemed as if it took hours. By the time my mom came home, three hours later, I was still in shock. I went to bed without eating.

The next day I make my way to the turf to tell Rod. Would you believe that bastard had the nerve to say it wasn't his and not to come around him with all that bull****. I can't believe this is happening to me. I proceed to walking home which is about a 20 minute walk. But I didn't care; I'm too pissed off and embarrassed to wait for the bus. Now what am I going to do? I don't have nothing or nobody. And I'm too ashamed to tell my mother. I went home and climbed up in my bed. I must have cried myself to sleep, because when I woke up my pillow was soaked. Lisa came by to see if I wanted to hang out, but I told her that I am pregnant and was just going to stay home tonight. Then she popped the question, "What are you going to do?" I told her I didn't know; I guess I'm going to get an abortion.

When I decided to go back to the clinic, I was three months pregnant. After telling the nurse practitioner that I wouldn't be keeping the baby, she gave me the information on how to get a free abortion. On the way home from the clinic, I saw a friend of mine in the car with her boyfriend. They ask me where I am going. I said, "Home." Then they asked if I would like to hang out with them. I say yes. As we were riding, he begins to complain about how his ex-girlfriend is pregnant and refuses to have an abortion even though he doesn't want the baby. Then he said something that changed my life forever. He said, "One thing about that girl is when she makes up her mind, she sticks to it." Something about hearing those words made me decide to keep my baby regardless of what Rod said or did. And the same way I made my mind up to keep the baby, is the same way he made his mind up to stop dealing with me all together. He was so serious that he didn't even speak to me when he saw me. He informed everybody on the turf that the baby wasn't his. It didn't take my mother long to notice the weight gain. She wasn't happy about it, but what was she going to say? I had already had an abortion, so she was hesitant to suggest another one. By the time I turned four months, the morning sickness was gone. So I was free to hang out again, but I didn't return to the turf due to embarrassment. As time went on, Lisa and I kind of drifted apart. I eventually called on an old friend named Lana. Lana was older than I and already had a two-year-old son, so she shared information with me about being pregnant. On days when she wasn't working, we would either hang out at her mom's house or my mom's house watching movies all day. One day when Lana and I were chilling at the house, the phone rang. It was Rod's mom telling me that he had been shot. When I arrived at the hospital, I found Rod's mom in the waiting room. She told me that he had been shot in the upper part of his arm and because the arm was extended forward when the bullet hit, it ripped through some muscles before exiting through his wrist causing severe damage. While we are talking, the doctor comes out to say that we can go in to see him, but that he would have to remain there about three days.

I sat alongside his bed all that day but he never woke up. I returned the next morning to visit. He woke up and saw me and asked how I knew he was there. I told him someone had given his mom my number and that I had met her yesterday and told her that I was pregnant. He was in so much pain that he didn't even respond. After four days, they decided to send him home, but he would have little or no usage of his arm for a while. So his mother tells him to come home with her until he feels better. Then she extends the invitation to me to join him. He doesn't say anything, so I accept the invite. Now, it's off to my mom's to pack. I must admit I am excited to be going with him to his mom's house.

After an hour drive to San Jose, CA, we finally arrive to his mom's house. It is a two bedroom apartment that she shares with her husband and daughter; so, that puts us on the living room sofa bed. One night while watching TV, he asks to see my stomach. While rubbing my stomach, his mother walks in. She looks at me and says that one day when she came by the turf looking for Rod, a girl told her that I was pregnant but the baby wasn't Rod's. I assured her that the girl was lying and that this is his baby. So she proceeds into the kitchen to get something to drink and return to her room. I become very emotional and turn over to try to go to sleep. Rod apologizes for what his mom said and tells me not to worry about anything. "We'll just see when the baby comes." *Hold the hell up! It's funny that nobody was saying this when I was sitting at the hospital with him from sun up to sun down. If he really felt like this, why didn't he tell me to leave the hospital? And...they both should not have let me come out here with them. It's cool though, because I can always go back home.*

Well it's early August and I am turning five months. Rod is doing better and has started back to driving himself to the bay area to hang on turf with his friends. I have decided to go back home where I belong. It doesn't make much sense for me to be sleeping on a sofa bed when I got a bed at home. Plus, Rod is starting to stay out all night, leaving me alone at his parents. Now that I have returned back home and him back to the turf, it's been two months since we've seen each other.

Here I am, now seven months pregnant, with no money, no car, all alone, and catching the bus to the doctor every Friday feeling like a failure. No one to share my hurt with, no one to feel the baby kick, and no one to listen to the heart beat with me. How did I end up like this? What happened to going to college after high school? Why hadn't anyone been there to guide me?

A few weeks later, I get a call from my attorney telling me to come to his office to pick up a $300 check from when my ankle got broke. I go and get the check and on the way home, I stop off at the check cashing place, and cash it. As I'm holding the money in my hand, I realize that it's not much. So I begin to think about how I can multiply it. Then a light goes off in my head. I hop on a bus and head to a local car wash which is being used as a front to deal drugs. There I hook up with an old friend and cop (buy) an eight ball of powder cocaine, nominating myself as a drug dealer. I continue on home and while my mom is still away at work, I call over a known drug addict and have her transform the powder cocaine into crack. Now I am open for business. Within weeks I have addicts tapping on my bedroom window all day and night for crack. Money is rolling in non-stop. I've bought new furniture for my room, began to buy baby clothes, and have even been able to save some money.

Then one day out of the blue, Rod calls. Yep, the Rod I haven't seen or heard from in two months. He calls to give me a number that I can reach him at when I go into labor. While I got him on the phone, I ask him to give me $150 dollars to purchase a baby bed. Surprisingly, he says, "Yes." So I make plans immediately to go and collect money from him.

Lana and I are still hanging tough. She is much more mature than my other friends. She likes to hang out, but because she knows that I have to hang at the house for my customers, she stays at the house with me watching movies all day.

Well ya'll, it's December 31st, and my due date has come and gone, with still no baby. New Year's Eve is here and everyone is excited and making plans to go out; I'm home sitting here on the couch, alone, watching TV, and waiting for the ball to drop in Times Square.

Who Cried For The Little Girl

It's 6:00 a.m., Monday, January 6, 1986, and I'm awaken with what I'm thinking is gas pain. I hear my mom in the other room preparing for work, but I'm afraid to tell her what's going on. I wait about two hours; then I call Lana. She immediately jumps in her car to come and take me to the hospital. By the time we reach the hospital, I am three centimeters; so, they admit me. By 7:00 p.m., my contractions are five minutes apart. So I decide to have Lana call Rod. He comes to the hospital right away. After being in labor for 26 hours, the doctor decides that he wants to do a c-section. As they begin to prep me for surgery, Rod looks at the doctor and asks him if he could come in the operating room. The doctor looks up at him and tells him he needs to ask me. I was in so much pain; I couldn't have said no if I wanted to. Plus, I didn't want to; I was glad he was there. So I shook my head 'yes'.

About 9:00 a.m., I awake from surgery to find out I have given birth to a 9lb, 14oz baby boy. They transferred me to the maternity ward and brought the baby in to me. By this time, Lana and Rod have gone home to get some rest. Later on that evening, Rod returns to the hospital with his mom. She takes one look at the baby and says, "Rod, he looks just like you when you were born." No, I didn't jump for joy or wave the victory flag; this wasn't new news to me. I didn't need her stamp of approval. I knew he was the daddy. The doctor comes in to tell me that I would have to remain in the hospital for five days due to the surgery. Rod and his mom soon leave, leaving me all alone with this baby. I'm looking at this big, ole baby thinking how cute he is. He has a head full of black, thick, curly hair, a long, pointy chin, super, fat cheeks, and some bright, brown eyes. Tears began to fall down my cheeks and I squeeze him close to my chest.

It's Saturday, and my five days are up. It's time for me to leave the hospital, and I haven't seen Rod since the day the baby was born. Lana picks me up from the hospital, takes me home, and helps baby and me get settled in. Thanks to all the money I made from selling crack, my room is completely furnished with everything to make baby and me comfortable. The next morning, which is Sunday, Lana arrives early to bathe

Baby Mama Drama

baby while I get freshened up. While I'm in the shower, she knocks on the door to tell me that Rod is banging on the front door. I tell her not to open it; I will be there in a minute. I hurry to get dressed and rush to the door. I crack the front door open and ask him what does he want? He says he wants to see his baby. I say, "Your baby?" Then I remind him of how he treated me when I told him that I was pregnant, and the words that his mama spoke to me when I was staying at her house. So he and I go back and forth in words. Then he tells me that he has a cab waiting on him. I say, "Good! Go jump in it!" Then I shut the door. About a minute later, he bangs on the door again. I open it and say, "What?" He is standing there with his arms full of shopping bags, with the cab driver coming up the stairs behind him with four cases of baby milk. He comes in all excited about what he has bought the baby and asks can he visit with him for a while? Of course I let him stay; he's my baby daddy.

After a few months, we begin dating again. By now, my body has healed and my son is healthy and growing fast. I can't believe he will be one-year-old in a few months. And his grandmother was right; he does look just like his daddy. Speaking of his daddy, everything between us seems to be going good; we're even talking about moving into our own place. He comes to my mom's and spends the night with baby and me at least three times a week. During those nights Rod spent with me, he became bothered by the fact that the majority of the drug seekers who were at my window during the night were men. And it was not long before he asked me to stop selling drugs all together, with the promise that he would give me money every week. So I stopped selling drugs. We have decided to rent an apartment. We move into a townhouse in Castro Valley, CA, about 20 minutes away from Oakland. It's a two bedroom, two bath place. It's extremely nice. We go out and buy new furniture for the entire house. We invite a few friends over to celebrate and everything is well. I'm playing the loving mother and wife, and he is playing the father and happy husband. We are in our place for about five months when all hell breaks out. I decide to answer his beeper one morning while he is asleep.

It's a female saying that she is pregnant by him. I immediately wake him up and question him. He says that she is lying, that she saw him one day driving his cousin's drop top BMW, and thinks that he has a lot of money and is just trying to get some. So I tell him to get dressed and take me to her house so he can confront her. Like a fool he does. We leave our house and drive to Oakland. When we get to her mother's house, we all go in. I begin to ask her to go into detail about their supposed relationship. She says that one night they hooked up and had sex and now she is pregnant. He begins to say that he is not the father and begins to name other guys that she slept with. I then turn to him and ask him one question, "Did you have sex with her?" He said yes. I grab my two-year-old son's hand and walk back to the car. While riding, we argue for about 15 minutes. When he pulls up to a stop sign, I grab my baby and hop out of the car. He tries to talk me into getting back in, but I refuse. I continue to walk, heading in the direction of my mom's house. While walking, I pass an Asian girl, out in her yard, watering the grass. She sees how upset I am and ask me if I need a ride. I gladly accept. When I enter my mother's house, I know right away that this is where I will be for a while. As matter of fact, I never should have left, but foolishly, I ignored all the signs in the beginning of the relationship that let me know that we wouldn't make it. See this wasn't the first time that Rod had gotten caught in some mess with a female. There was another incident when my son was a few months old and I caught Rod with a female friend of mine. I went to jail for busting her head open with a wine bottle.

So the next day, I return to the townhouse to collect all of my son's and my clothing. Unfortunately, big Rod and I don't work out. After the split, I find out that he has been smoking crack and cheating on me with several different females for over a year. But I no longer care; I have become numb to his foolishness. I start back selling crack at my mom's house and am so self sufficient that being without him doesn't really faze me. As a matter of fact, I realize that I really never needed him. I soon move in with a friend and purchase me a new car. I sometimes ride through his old drug turf and find him there looking bad with dirty clothes and in need of a haircut. So, once I took him to my house to shower and get a bite to eat, only to return him back to the turf.

I eventually meet a guy from another part of the city and he has my full attention. He's kind to me and enjoys spending time with my son who will be turning three very soon. He's even giving my son a nickname; he calls him "Rod Slick" because he is always sneaking candy. So after a few months of dating, we decide to move in together. A month after the move, we decide to tell everyone that I was two months pregnant. He and I are very excited because he has no kids. But our excitement doesn't last long. By the time I reached three months, I start suffering from severe abdominal pain. Early one morning, he rushes me to the emergency room where they discover that I have gone into shock from abdominal bleeding and that my blood pressure is extremely low. The doctor informs us that the baby is in my fallopian tube and it has ruptured. If I stayed home another hour, I would have died. As I lie there listening to the doctor, all I could think about was the abortion that I had. They decide to perform an emergency surgery, and after two blood transfusions and a week-long stay in the hospital, they send me home. My boyfriend is devastated; he is so hurt that he is scared to touch me. I went from 150lbs to 110lbs; I am pale and can't walk without holding onto the wall. It takes me about four months for things to get back to normal around the house. They get normal, but not better. Within three months, he gets busted for drugs and sent to jail for 10 months. Even though I visit for a few months, the relationship doesn't survive.

Lana and I continue to hang tough. With her job and my dope money, we stay in the latest fashions and party at least three days a week. One night, when leaving a neighborhood club, we decide to hitch a ride with a friend and go to the after hour club. While at the club, we both decide that we are ready to go home. But unfortunately, the person that we rode with isn't ready to go. So, I ask my baby daddy's cousin Robert if he can drop us back to my car. He says he was riding with a friend, but he can have her give us a ride. When we exit the after hour's club, there is a guy on a bicycle posted on the corner. We walk by him and proceed to cross the street. When the four of us reach the middle of the street, we hear gunfire. Robert and the girl proceed to run across the street, but Lana and I run back towards the club, not knowing that the shooting is being done by the guy on the bike. He is shooting at Robert who is a well-known drug dealer. Once back inside the after hour club, I become concerned about Robert. So, I decide to go out and look for him to make sure he has not been shot. I begin walking in the direction that I last saw him run in and begin to call his name. I find him hiding on the side of a house. I walk over to him to make sure that he is alright. When I get to him, we see the headlights of a car slowly approaching, so we both duck down in some bushes. I then reach in my purse and hand him my 25 automatic pistol. When the car drives by, we see a guy hanging from the window with a tech 9 gun, which holds approximately 20 rounds. I am breathing so hard that Robert puts his hand over my mouth. Once the car passes, I tell him to keep the gun and that I am going to get a car to get him out of here. I return back to the club and tell Lana what just happen and that I need to get a car. I find the friend that we rode with to the after hour club and tell her that I need her car for an emergency but will be right back. I tell Lana that I need her to come with me. I drive back to where Robert is, pick him up, and go back to the neighborhood club to get my car. When we reach my car, I tell Robert to take the car and that I will follow him to his house. Once he gets home, I collect my gun and car and then return my friend's car. Lana and I then go to my house, where we replay the chain of events until we fall asleep.

Chapter 5

I Do

One Friday night, I decide to hit the club by myself. I get showered and put on my size 30 designer jeans with a snug fitting shirt. My hair is hanging straight, reaching just a little below my bra strap, and every strand is in place. My make-up is perfect with my ruby red lipstick. While standing at the bar, a guy comes up and makes a joke about the people on the dance floor. I smile and we begin to converse. His name is Demetrius. Demetrius is a caramel toned brother, about 5'11" with a thin body frame, deep dimples, and a cute smile. We exchange numbers and go our separate ways. A few days later, Demetrius gives me a call asking when he can see me again. I tell him that I have a boyfriend, but we are in the process of breaking up. Then to my surprise, he tells me that he has a girlfriend. But I still allow Demetrius to keep phoning me and periodically meet up with him at different clubs to talk. Then one night, we decide to hook up; I mean really hook up. We drive far out to get a motel room, to avoid any running into our mates. But that only last for so long. As we get closer, we got sloppy. One night, while Demetrius and I sit in local club, my soon to be ex-boyfriend walks in. He tells me to get up from the table and go home. I look at him with a look of disgust, but due to the violent history of our relationship, I immediately get up and out. On my way driving home, I ask myself a very important question: *did I just get caught slipping, or had I already walked away from the relationship in my heart?* The answer was simple. Normally I drive out far to meet Demetrius, but tonight, I met him at a club five minutes from my house and parked my car in plain view. I had emotionally walked out of the relationship. By the time we reach my one bedroom apartment, he is steaming. As soon as we get in the door, he slaps me and throws me on the couch. He is kicking my furniture and breaking up my things; so, I run out the door and call the police. By the time the police arrive, he is gone. So I phone Demetrius to tell him what just happened. He feels so bad that he decides to come and get me so we can go to a motel for he doesn't want me spending the night alone. He comes up with a lie to tell his girlfriend about having to be away for the night. I finally reach a decision that night to end my current relationship and pursue one with Demetrius.

But by me being single, I have more time to spend with Demetrius. However, that put more pressure on him and a strain on his relationship with his girlfriend. After a month of us constantly spending time together, his girlfriend moves out of their place and back to her mom's house. So Demetrius and I become an item. We take turns spending the night at each other's house, to where eventually, he decides to just move into my place. After five months of dating, we decide to go to Reno, Nevada to do some gambling and catch a show. While having a good time eating and drinking, we found ourselves at a wedding chapel saying, "I do." Yep, we got married; no rings, no wedding gown, no flowers, no cake, just us standing before a minister. We return home the next day and tell our families. Everyone is shocked—I mean eyes bucked out their heads shocked. But we didn't care. We go to our little place and call it a night. Two months later, Demetrius informs me that he had caught a drug case the previous year and the judge has sentenced him to four months in a half-way house. So I vowed to stay by his side until he got out. Well ya'll, after running to the half-way house for two months, and taking care of Demetrius's business and mine, I was tired. So I cut back on the visits and phone calls, and begin to make plans to take care of me. And in the process of taking care of me, I start to date my old boyfriend again. Yep, the one I left for Demetrius. Things are going great, we are laughing again, and sharing our hearts with one another; it feels good. So good, that I have not gone to see Demetrius in a month. I have only talked to him maybe four times. He knows something is up, but he just can't quite put his finger on it. I inform my new, old boyfriend of Demetrius's release date, and that Demetrius will have to come here for his things, but that will be the extent of our relationship. Two weeks before Demetrius's release, I go to the court house and file for an annulment and the judge grants it right on the spot. I am a free woman now. So when Demetrius comes out, I will inform him of the divorce and that he needs to get his belongings from my house. Call me wrong, mean and cruel. I don't care; he is getting out!

Now I know that sounds harsh and unfair, but before you close the book on me, Demetrius ain't been no saint ya'll. I found out that he is still communicating with his ex-girlfriend and has even snuck to see her one day with flowers in hand, while he had me running for him like a courier service.

Two more days and I will be free completely from Demetrius. I guess I'll grab myself a glass of wine—better yet a shot of gin. Wouldn't you know it, right in the middle of my celebration, the phone ring. It's my new, old boyfriend saying that he is in jail for a warrant on a drug charge with no bail. What the hell? We had plans to be to together. Now what? I must have taken about seven shots of gin back to back until I could barely see. Then, I went to bed.

Demetrius is calling all excited about being released, and I am in mourning. My new, old boyfriend calls to say that they are not releasing him; he will be there 120 days. 120 days? That's four months! Now what in the hell is really going on? My plan was to leave Demetrius and hook back up with him and now he's gone. I don't know if a drink will help today. I might need some sleeping pills to get through this day.

Demetrius is calling needing a ride home; so, I force myself to go and get him. Upon arriving back at the house, he can tell that something is bothering me, but he never asked what. As the day comes to an end, I fix him something to eat and then go to take a shower. While I'm in the shower, the phone rings and Demetrius answers it. It's a collect call from my new, old boyfriend. I hear Demetrius arguing with him. I come out of the bathroom, snatch the phone out of Demetrius's hand, and hang it up. Then he has the audacity to question me about whom that was on the other line. I tell him to get out of my face and that this is my house. "Don't ever question me about who is calling my phone." We argue for about five minutes. Then I walk to a drawer and give him the divorce papers. I tell him to get his stuff so I can drop him off to his parents' house. My nerves are already bad and the last thing I need is him in my face with some bullcrap. He looks at me puzzled in a state of disbelief. Then I begin to tell him that I know all about him parading to his ex-girlfriend's job with flowers and her visiting him in the half-way house. "Boom!" That wipes that "state of confusion" look off his face quickly. I must have driven about 80 mph trying to drop him off at his parents' house. Neither one of us said a word in the car. He couldn't even close the door all the way before I pulled off. After that night, we never spoke or saw each other again. Thank God.

So here I am, single for the first time since I was in the third grade. And I have nothing but time on my hands. So I register to become a foster parent and start a family home daycare to generate some income. I also begin to hang out at a club called Apt. C in the evenings and developed an addiction for shooting darts. Before I know anything, I'm in the club at least three nights a week. It's really fun and I have met a lot of new friends. One night while minding my own business, I meet a guy named Cory, who is also a lover of darts. And we begin to hang out together every night, shooting darts in different clubs. Cory is an excellent dart player and everyone on the dart circuit knows him. And now they are trying to figure out who this hot, new chick on the set is. After a couple of weeks of hanging out together, we begin to date. Cory, at the time, is living with a roommate, so he hangs out at my house all the time. At the present time, Cory is unemployed and looking for a job. He also has two young boys that he rarely mentions or visits (red flag).

I have completed my foster care and daycare class, and have been licensed by the state to operate as a business. Upon receiving my license, I get a call to place a newborn, bouncing baby boy in my home fulltime. Things are looking up for my good. But with the good also comes the bad. I then receive a phone call from my dad, asking me had I talked with my mother. I said no. He says that she had phoned him in an up rage about him telling one of my sisters that he wasn't my dad. I tell him that I know nothing about it. When we hang up, I immediately think about a conversation that I once had with a family friend shortly after I turned 18. I heard rumors that he wasn't my dad, and that the man who fathered one of my sisters was actually my dad. Although I never questioned my parents about it, I did recall in the 3rd grade when they began testing all the African American students at my school for sickle cell anemia. My sister and I both tested positive for the trait; but, neither of my parents had it. One of those things that make you go, "Hum!" So I phone my sister, Pam, to see what is going on, and she tells me that she is tired of my mom's lies, and that she had told my mom that I knew who my real dad was and that I had known about him for years. So my mom assumed my dad had told me, and that prompted her to phone him. After speaking with my sister for about 20 minutes, we decide to phone another sister, Denise, and share with her how my mom went off on my dad. So now you have three angry heifers on the phone. Out of anger, we all meet up, hop in my car, and drive to my older sister's house where my mom is, visiting. When we arrive, both twins are there sitting, watching TV with my mom. We tell my mom that there are some things that she needs to clear up about our past, so that we may know the truth and find some peace. We sat there and questioned my mom for hours about all the sexual abuse that we had experienced, and she sternly looked at us and said, "I never knew about anyone being molested." We begin to question her more aggressively. "We were little girls! How did you not know that we were being raped? Our behaviors had to change. There had to be stains in our underwear," we said in frustration. She then said she never saw any evidence in our underwear or notice any change in our behaviors. I am sitting there stunned! When I questioned her about my dad, she said, "I never told him that he was your dad." I said, "Huh? What you mean you never told him that he was my dad? Did he know that you were involved with someone else, and that there was a possibility that he might not be my dad?" She said that she and my dad had lost contact while she was pregnant, and that after I was born, her friend had ran into him one day and told him that she had given birth to his baby. So when they finally hooked backed up, he just assumed that I was his, and she never told him any different. Then I said, "But you knew that I wasn't his because my sister and I, who are supposed to have different dads, look like twins and neither one of us look like the man who I have been calling daddy. Before she could respond, one of my twin sisters commented to her defense saying, "Well, you know mom is old now and a lot of that stuff she don't really remember." So I say to her,

"Well, she needs to try to remember because this stuff has put us in an unhealthy mental state. Things that had been suppressed from childhood have resurfaced, and that as an adult I am finding it extremely difficult to function. I'm having bad dreams, running from man to man, and finding myself depressed even when things are going good. So in order for me to move on, I need some answers to my question. I need to know who I am, and what happened to me to make me do things that I do? Why don't I like to wear dresses; why did I stop wanting to hug and kiss my dad at five-years-old; why am I so over protective with my son; why am I so revengeful and bitter? I came here for answers, not to be lied to. So she needs to remember! And further more I would appreciate it if you would let mom speak for herself!"

The three of us must have stayed there for over three hours questioning my mom, and re-playing situations and conversations as if it had happened yesterday. And her only response was that she knew nothing of the molestations and that she had never lied to any of us about who our fathers were, because we never asked her. See I wasn't the only one who didn't know who her father was. My other sister, Denise, who had come with me, had been lied to also about her dad. All I could do was shake my head in disbelief. So we left the way we came—angry. I returned home, took a shower, poured me some gin, and passed out to sleep.

After six months of dating, Cory says to me that he thinks it would be best if he just moved in with me since he's here almost every night. So he comes by the next day with a small bag containing his belongings (2nd red flag). Well, Cory has now been here for about five months and things seem to be going good. As a matter of fact, we will be attending one of my high school friend's wedding today. So I'm super excited to be attending the wedding in the company of a man and not just with my girlfriends. Cory and I are having a good time at the wedding; he even caught the garter at the reception. That garter must have been good luck because a week didn't go by and Cory asked me to marry him. Of course, I said yes. We broke the news to my family and immediately set a wedding date for July 19, 1997. My sisters were so excited that they all came over with pens and notebooks to start planning the wedding.

Two weeks later while at home relaxing, my girlfriend, whom had just recently married, calls me. She calls me to say that while showing a co-worker her wedding photos, one of them recognizes Cory and says that he is already married to her friend. What? I know this Negro has not been here all this time, up in my face, and he's married. I begin to pace the floor while waiting on him to come home. As soon as he opens the door, I begin to question him about what I heard. He just looks at me like he has seen a ghost. When the shock wears off, he begins to tell me that yes, he is married, but he plans to file for divorce and expects it to be final before our wedding day. He then says the reason he withheld the information was because he was afraid that he would lose me (3rd red flag). So the next day, we both go down to legal aid to file his divorce papers. Now with that being taken care of, I feel better. So we continue on with the wedding plans. I find the perfect wedding dress; I rent the hall, hire the caterer, and the party planner will handle the rest.

Saturday, July 19th has finally arrived, and everything is falling into place. While sitting waiting to have my make up applied, I see a shadow walk by the window. I look out and it's Cory walking up with his groomsmen. And as I look at him walking by, I know in my heart that I have no business marrying him. But I go through with it anyway. I do it, not because I love him and want to spend the rest of my life with him. I marry him to save face, and because I have already spent 30,000 dollars of my money on this day.

The wedding goes on without a hitch. Everybody is excited and having a good time. I'm even smiling to make everyone think that I am happy. But inside, I feel terrible.

The next day, Cory and I return to my apartment. He still has no job, but has decided to go back to school and look for part-time work. Believe it or not, I am still selling crack. However, I don't allow customers at my house; I only make home deliveries now. I also decided to go to school to learn a trade. So we are both taking morning classes, and Cory works now in the evenings at his school. So, again, everything seems to be going well, until one night at our favorite club, an older gentleman comes up to me and asks if he could speak with me. We step outside and he begins to tell me that while I am in the club shooting darts, Cory is next door at the wash house with the young, female attendant. Then he begs me not to tell Cory that the information came from him. I agree to keep him anonymous. I return back in the club to have a drink and continue to play darts. About 30 minutes into the game, Cory tells me that he is going outside with a friend to smoke some weed and that he will be right back. I wait about five minutes and go outside to look for him. It doesn't take long for me to find him. I walk right next door to the wash house and there he is, leaning all over the counter, and smiling in the face of the young, female attendant. I walk up behind him and ask him, "What are you doing?" He storms out of the wash house, heading to his car. I jump in front of him and we begin to argue. I'm questioning him about what is going on and he is lying saying, "Nothing." I hop into my car and go home. Cory never comes home or calls. The next day, he shows up and apologizes for the way things looked, and assures me that he has never had any relations with the young attendant. I, in my foolish state of mind, allow him to stay.

I Do

    Cory and I will soon be celebrating our one-year anniversary and although it hasn't been peaches and cream, we are still together. We still hang out three or four times a week shooting darts. Next week, we will be traveling out of town to a dart tournament in Sacramento, CA, and I can't wait; my local team will be playing the championship game.

    Cory and I make it safely to Sacramento; and, you can literally feel the excitement when you enter the ball room. People and dart boards are everywhere. I have hooked up with my team mates and we have won the first four games and are on our way to the finals to bring home the first place trophy. There's only one problem; I can't find Cory to give him the good news. I call his phone—no answer. I check the room; he's not there. I ask friends and no one has seen him. I search the whole ballroom looking for him, and then I begin to race through the lobby. Still no sign of Cory. Something tells me to check the hotel restaurant. When I do, I find him leaning on the counter, all smiled up in the young hostess's face. I tap him on the back and ask him what's up? He walks past me trying to exit the restaurant before I embarrass him. We begin to argue in the lobby, but before we can finish, they call my name on the intercom asking me to return back to the ballroom to play my final match of darts. I return back to the ballroom and Cory goes towards the elevator. My team wins the final match and goes on stage to get our trophy and as I look into the audience, no Cory. After taking pictures, I go to the room to look for Cory and he has packed his bag and left. So I pack my stuff and make the long drive back home alone. I didn't see or hear from Cory for two days. Finally, he calls to say that he has been staying with his dad. We talk on the phone for a few hours, ending the conversation with him saying that he was sorry and would return home tomorrow.

    Tomorrow came and so did Cory. But something was different—not with him, but with me. Even though he is back, I still feel lost and confused. So much so that as I am sitting on the couch watching my foster daughter struggle to open the patio door, I contemplate going out and jumping over the balcony. But before I can turn the thought into an action, she walks away from the door frustrated about not being able to open it. A few days go by and I'm sitting home alone watching Oprah and there's a lady on there by the name of Iyanla Vanzant. She is discussing her book, *In the meantime.* I rush out to get the book . In the book, she keeps referring to a higher power, which I take means "God". As I am reading it, it begins to speak to my heart. And it's at that moment that I realize that something is missing in my life. There's a hole in my soul that I have been trying to fill with men, money, and a good time, only to still end up empty. So I decide to go to church.

Sunday morning comes and I get up, get dressed, and make my way to church. It was good, so I told myself that I would be back next week. When next week came, I went back. And I went back again and again. The more I went to church the less time I had to hang out shooting darts. I would stay home and watch TV while Cory went out almost every night. I received several phone calls telling me that he was in the clubs hanging out with different females, but for some strange reason I couldn't muster up the strength to even question him about it. His behavior went on for months and I just kept going to church. He even offered to go with me one Sunday, but I strongly urged him not to. I didn't want anyone seeing me with him. Returning home from church one Sunday morning, I heard the Lord clearly say to me, 'Tell him he has to leave now." I walked into the bedroom where he was laying in bed, with my remote control in his hand, watching football. And I said to him, "In four weeks I need you to move out." Mind you, that was not what God told me to say. He looked at me and said, "I can leave right now." I whispered in my mind, "Sorry God for not saying it like you told me to, but thank you Jesus; he's leaving. He got up and began to pack and I helped him. He was dressed and all packed up within 30 minutes. And as I'm watching him leave, he is filling up the car with several bags of clothing and shoes. Then I thought back on the one small bag he had when he came and felt like a fool. But it's okay; I will feel like a fool by myself, because he is out of here! The next day, I went out and bought me a brand new bedroom set and linen. Then I drove over to the same legal aid firm that assisted him in the divorce from his previous wife and had them draw up divorce papers for us. And for the first time in my life, I had peace. I never shed one tear or felt the urge to call him once he left. What I later realized was that I had already divorced Cory in my heart and mind months before I asked him to leave. God had directed my steps and that was where the peace came from.

Cory and I never talked or saw each other again until the death of my father approximately eight months later. He came to the funeral. I believe he saw somebody different when he saw me, because he didn't even attempt to approach me. And it was not anger that he saw; I believe he saw that I was at peace. Cory and I never crossed paths again. It's true what they say, "When wrong people leave, right things happen. I continued to go to church and vowed to God that I would be in church every Sunday and Wednesday, pay my tithes, and give an offering. I would run my daycare and take care of my kids. My daycare is at full capacity, I have three foster kids, my son is in private school, I have a new car, and bringing in almost 10 grand a month. I had never felt so free in my life. I have arrived!

Chapter 6

Who Cried for the Little Girl?

❧❀☙

Well ya'll, I thought that I had arrived until one day while watching Oprah, she brings back well known author, Iyanla Vanzant, and she began talking about relationships. She was asking women, "What are you doing in the meantime? What do you do while you're single?" Then she began to share tips on dating, and how it's important that you get rid of all unnecessary baggage before entering into a relationship. As I sat there, I began to think about my life. I began to mentally ram shack my baggage. I thought about every relationship that I had been in; every bad decision that I had made; and all the hurt that I had caused others; all the hurt and abuse that I had been through; all the lives that I had helped to destroy with drugs; all the bad checks and illegal credit cards that I had stolen and used. As I thought about my life, I began to cry. Not just tears rolling, I cried as if someone had called and said my mama had died. I went into the bathroom to wipe my face and as I reached for a towel, I got a glimpse of my face in the mirror. I stopped and looked in the mirror, but when I looked in the mirror I didn't see a 32-year-old woman. I saw a six-year-old little girl with a white ribbon, holding a ponytail together at the top of her head, with a white, short-sleeved shirt, with some bright, brown eyes. And as I looked at her, I began to cry for her. And I wondered if anyone else had ever cried for her? When the tricycle fell on her head, did anyone lose any sleep over that or shed a tear? When she was raped in the back bedroom on the blue and white stripped mattress, did anyone see the stains in her underwear and cry at the thought of what could have happened to her? When her plaid skirt was kicked up in front of the school kids, did anyone of them go home crying and tell their parents? When she was raped in the bathroom on the pink carpet, did the other kids in the room cry as she yelled out for help? Did a teacher ever know that something wasn't right and cry for her? When she told the neighborhood teenage boys about what her brother did to her and they laughed, did any of them go home and cry feeling bad about laughing at her? When her sister failed to tell her mom about finding her in the closet, did she ever cry for not protecting her? When her body was covered with flea bites, did her mom silently cry from the disgust of not being able to ease her discomfort? When the teenage boy slapped her in junior high school, did anyone feel bad for her and cry? When she laid her head on the desk at the welfare office in need of an emergency medical card, did the worker go home and cry for the lost and confused teenage girl secretly trying to get an abortion? Did her mom cry when she found out that she was pregnant and was planning on having an abortion? Did the nurse who held her hand during the abortion cry when she got home after watching a young girl go through such a painful procedure? Did the father of the baby ever cry, for his participation and abandonment? After all the humiliation that Rod caused her during her pregnancy, did he ever cry for her? Did her mom go home and cry after she confronted her about who her real dad was?

Who cried for the little girl?

I cried for the little girl, and not only did I cry for the little girl, I also began to cry for the woman that she had become. What was it that made her turn out the way that she had? Was it the head injury, the abuse, the marijuana, the abortion? What was it?

To narrow it down to just one thing would be too easy. A wise man once said that our experiences shape us into who we are. And I believe that's what happened to me. A collection of my experiences turned me into a confused, lost, little girl trapped in a woman's body feeling hopeless. I'm feeling as if I just existed, but without a purpose. I mean really what had I accomplished? Yes I had a new car, some money in the bank, and was free from hazard relationships, but if I would have died the next day, what kind of example had I set for my son? What legacy did I leave behind? Was I a mom that he could be proud of? Here I was 32-years-old and feeling like I felt when I was 18 and pregnant—lost and lonely. What would it take for me to discover who I am? I know it looks to others like I am super confident about who I am, but it's hard to fool yourself. Because at the end of the day, when you dismantle, you have to face yourself. And although God had removed some people from my life that I thought I needed, I was still holding on to something. And it was something from my past. Had I become so infatuated with my past that I didn't want to let it go? What was happening to me? How is it that I'm back depressed and feeling suicidal? I go to church twice a week and give money. How can I be feeling like this?

And as I sat down on the side of the bath tub, I realized that my "then" was affecting my now. There was something from my past that had been suppressed and not identified and dealt with. I started questioning myself as to why had I been so promiscuous at an early age; was it the sex that I enjoyed or was it the idea of having someone? The answer became very clear; it was the idea of being loved, and I say the idea of being loved, because at that moment, I realized that I had never really experienced love. I had no idea of what love was. So I had been and was still running from man to man trying to find what I had no clue about. So I unknowingly identified love as sex. Sitting there on that tub, I couldn't think of one time as a kid ever hearing my parents, my sisters, or any other family member telling me that they loved me. I couldn't recall, not one time, my mother hugging me as a kid, or ever saying that she was proud of me. I never heard my father say that I was his pretty, little girl. I remember being told that whenever I saw my dad on the weekends, I was to hug him when I got there and hug him when I left his house. And even that didn't last long. Because at the age of five, I told him that I didn't want to hug him anymore, and he told my mom that I no longer had to. The times that we went to my dad's house, I never saw him and my mom hug or even exchange words of affection. Not only did I not see them, I had never seen my adult sisters hug or kiss their mates, or hear the words I love you being exchanged. How was I to mirror something that I had never seen? Boy was I messed up in the area of love! Not just in displaying it to a man, but also in my friendships. Because I had no clue that a real friendship would require love; so, I also had a lot of failed friendships. Not that I didn't genuinely enjoy their company, I just was clueless as to what a real friendship required. So when it came to being truthful and loyal to them, I failed. But how was I to get a passing grade in this area without ever hearing about it or seeing it displayed? My brothers never had friends; they were too busy fighting with each other or in jail. The only friends of my sisters that I had seen were the ones who would come to the house to party and drink with them. My mom's friends consisted of two people, and all they ever did was go to roller derby together. And although my sister, Pam and I were very close in age, we were not friends. We never hung around each other. We both had different sets of associates. We never talked about our feelings, about boys, about fashion; we were total opposites.

So as I'm sitting there, I'm realizing that I am messed up mentally! At this moment, the only person that I say that I truly love is my son. So I reflect back on how I was always kissing his cheeks as a baby and keeping him in bed with me, even though he had his own bed. I kept him close to me so that no one would harm him. I made sure he had the best of everything and vowed to put him in private school by the time he reached junior high school. But was that love or was that just protection and provision? Did I actually say the words, "I love you" or did I expect him to just know it by my actions? It's true; you can't give what you don't have, and you can't teach what you have not learned. So I had turned out to be the mother that I had. However, what I couldn't understand was why had all this come to surface now; why hadn't it been brought to my attention before? The answer was simple. Before I decided to go back to church and give my life to Christ, I was living according to what I saw and by what I believed in my own mind to be right. And whenever you set your own rules, you set yourself up for failure. See, although the thoughts of my short comings had been provoked by the Oprah show, it was the Holy Spirit which had taken up residency in my heart once I accepted Jesus as Lord and Savior, that was convicting and correcting me in that bathroom.

See, people had been so-called loving me and accepting me as I was, but the God who really loved me refused to let me marinate in my mess. And the bathroom was the perfect place to discard my mess. God had suppressed my past up until now, because He knew that if it had surfaced earlier, it would have killed me. So He waited until I reconciled back to him, putting me in a position to get the proper guidance that I would need to survive these memories. So I sat there and cried for a long time, then I finally got up, cleaned my face, and said, "Okay God. I'm ready; teach me how to love."

Then, as I was leaving the bathroom, God spoke to me. He said, "I need for you give to others what I have given to you." I paused and said, "Okay," and mentally I started forming a list of people of who I could give money too. He said, "Not money, give them what I have given you; give them My Word." By not fully understanding what God had said to me, the next day, I went to see the pastor of the church that I had been attending, and told him all about my bathroom (Damascus) experience. He said that God was calling me to preach, and with all that I had been through, he knew why. Then he said God was going to use me to reach thousands of women to encourage them to give their lives to Him. And I'm thinking as he is speaking, *I don't know a lot about the Bible.* He must have saw the confusion on my face because he said, "Just keep coming to church and God will release you when you're ready to do ministry."

I got in my car and drove home still not really understanding what was to come. About a week later, God told me to pack up all my party clothes and get rid of them. Yep that meant all of my leather hot pants with the matching leather bra's (child, I had a red set, a black set and a yellow set) and all my miniskirts and sexy dresses. So I emptied out a full-sized double door closet and dropped everything off to an old friend, and boy was that heifer happy. On the way home from dropping off the clothes, God told me to make sure that my son started attending church also. And just as I was getting over the fact that I had just given away thousands of dollars of clothes, He hit me with something else. He said cut your hair off. Wait a minute now! Hold on God because now I know you are tripping! My hair is healthy, shiny and reaching past my bra strap. Women get weaves to look like me. I need my hair. And boy what did I say that for? God said, "That's the problem; you think you need it to be you. But I need you to get rid of it so you can become who I want you to become." The next night, which was a Friday, I walked upstairs from my apartment with scissors in my hand and asked my neighbor to cut my hair off. And she did it without question, cutting it down to about four inches long. The next morning, I got up early and went to the hair salon to have two more inches cut and to have it styled. I won't lie to you and say that I was happy about it because I wasn't, but I just smiled as if I was. *God I don't know what this is all about and I don't like it. I'm just doing it because you told me to, and to be honest, I'm so lost and confused, I don't know what else to do.* After being in church for a few months, I began notice that songs in church were causing me to cry, and hearing other people give their testimony was really reaching my heart. And my 13-year-old son was noticing the changes in me also. One day on the way home from church, he looked at me and said, "Child, you have gone from fighting people to crying in church," and laughed. I just looked at him and shook my head because I knew that God was softening my heart.

I started making more time to read my Bible other than at church, and things in it were beginning to make sense. So one day, as I was doing my daily reading, I stopped and asked God why was He closer to other people than to me? And He said, "I'm close to you too; you're just not close to me. You're coming to church and giving money, but you haven't surrendered your heart and mind to me. There is still some stuff in you that I have to break you from. That's why I had you get rid of the clothes and cut your hair, because those things don't make you; they just enhance who you already are. But you have been letting them define you. So I have to uncover the woman that I created you to be and in order to do that, you have to be broken." God said, "I'm moving you beyond believing in me; you have to get to know me and that comes from experience." I'm thinking, *what else is there for me to experience? Haven't I been through enough already? I wish you would have come along when I was a kid and maybe you wouldn't have to deal so harsh with me now.* And before I could finish, something came to mind that I had read in the Bible, "God knows what I am going to say, before I say it", and boy how true was this because before I could finish complaining about how God wasn't there when I was experiencing all my turmoil as a kid, He rudely interrupted my thoughts and said, "I knew you before you entered your mother's womb. I knew what would happen to you, who would do it, and when it would be done. He said, "A strand of hair doesn't leave your head without me knowing it." Then he went on to say that when the handle bar of the bike was dropped on my head, that although it hurt me, He didn't let it kill me. When I was being molested, it was him who caused the phone to ring stopping the action of the perpetrator. Even after the abortion, when I lay down in pain that night with tears in my eyes, it was him who had dried my eyes and given me the strength to return to school and graduate. Although my son's father had denied him, he (God) stood by me and gave me a healthy baby. When other drug dealers were being robbed and killed, he protected me even in my wrong. When I went to jail and the judge let me go, knowing I was guilty of all counts, there were other women who had gone through what I had been through. Some had lost their minds, some became drug addicts or had even lost their lives, and yet I was still standing clothed and in my right mind—with a place to stay, financially stable and a chance to get right. He said, "I was there then and I'm still here!" Everything in life can't be all good and no bad, somebody has to endure some pain so that they may come back and strengthen others. He said, "I trusted you with the trials because I knew that I could count on you to testify about them so that I would get the glory and others won't live such a defeated life. I allowed so much to happen to you, to place you on a larger platform so that thousands of women would be healed by your story."

He said, "You don't just need to learn how to love; you have to be made whole." I said, "I am whole." He said, "No you're not. Turn your Bible to John chapter five and read it." So I did; then he said, "This man had been sick for 38 years and felt that he couldn't get well because he had no one to put him in the water where he thought he needed to be for healing. But Jesus comes along and asked him, "Do you want to be made whole?" The man says, "I have no one to put me in the water to be healed." Jesus says, "Rise up and take that mat that you have been lying on and walk," and immediately the man was made whole. He picked up his mat and walked." I said, "Okay, but I already can walk; I'm not sick." He said, "You're not physically ill, but you are mentally." Then the scripture came alive. If Jesus would have just healed the man's leg, making him able to walk, he could have walked into some places or some situations that may have caused him to be worse off than he had been. But when He made him whole, He healed his mind, body, and soul.

So how does this relate to my situation? Simply, if God, who is Love, teaches me to accept His agape (unconditional) love, then I, in turn, can share that love with others. And one of the ways of teaching me how to love was to fully accept and understand how much He loves me. So that would take care of my love issue, but wouldn't help with the thoughts of depression or suicide. Because there are a lot of loving people in cemeteries or sanitariums. So when He says I need to be made whole, he's talking about a transformation. Heal the total person, because it does me no good to have a loving heart and a bad mind. So not only do I need to learn how to love, but I also need to know how to let go of things I have no control of. See, what I didn't realize was that my not knowing how to love just didn't affect my dealings in relationships, it left a hole in my heart that had become filled with anger, unworthiness, and depression. And I unknowingly had allowed those three characteristics: anger, unworthiness, and depression, to govern my life. But my anger was subtle; it didn't always show up in a loud and aggressive manner. It would sometimes manifest in a devious or revengeful way. The unworthiness kept me locked into relationships with men, who would physically abuse me, cheat on me, or constantly lie to me. It even had me spending thousands of dollars providing for them and I knew that they were not good to or for me. After living out these two characteristics, along with my childhood experiences, that itself explains how depression played a major role in my life.

So unlike the man who had an ailment for 38 years, who never answered when Jesus asked him if he wanted to be made whole, I'm answering God, "Yes make me whole."

He (God) said, "Then the first thing you need to do is forgive yourself. Call out all of the things that you have permitted to enter your life that you knew were hazardous and apologize to yourself. Then seek my forgiveness on behalf of those who you have wronged." So I began to write out a list or should I say a short novel and I called each one out in prayer. As I called them out, my body began to feel empty; I felt the heaviness leave my heart. When I got to the end of the list, the Holy Spirit said, "Pick back up the pen." So I did and I was led to write down all the good qualities that I did possess and those that I wanted to have. So when I stood up from praying, although I was crying, it wasn't that same depressing cry. I actually felt a sense of release. I now know that, that release is called peace. I had given it all to God. Now Satan no longer had anything to dangle in my face to use as a weapon to keep me handcuffed to my past. I was free from shame, embarrassment, and guilt.

Then God said, "Now take responsibility of your experiences and turn it around for some good."

I said, "Okay God, I'm just going to ride this out and see where it takes me." And after saying that, I didn't hear from God for a while. So by not knowing what to do next, I just kept doing what I had been doing: going to church, paying my tithes and offering, and reading at least three chapters a day in the Bible. Before I knew it, I would find myself in the grocery store and at the hair salon telling people about Jesus—about who He is and how He saved me. Not just how He physically saved me, but how He saved my soul from hell. And believe it or not, they were listening. They were amazed at all of the "stuff" that I had been through and now, I was going to church and the building hadn't burned down.

One Sunday morning while attending church, my son decided to give his life to Christ and said that he wanted to be baptized. Ya'll I cried like the world was coming to an end. I was so happy. So the next week, I invited my family and a few of my friends from the club to come to the baptism. And surprisingly, everyone came. But not only did they see my son get baptized, they also saw a different side of me. They saw me without all the designer clothes, the new hair cut, and hands lifted toward heaven, thanking God for letting me make it this far. They were puzzled as to what happened to me to make me decide to come to church. So I truthfully told them that the Oscar award person that they knew was really a lost and confused person. I had to make some changes before I ended up in a mental ward. Then I began to tell them how God had been protecting me through everything that I had been through, and that I had not gotten by this far because I was so lucky, crafty, or slick, but that God was saving me for such a time as this. They were like, "Wow, you even talk different." I didn't tell them it that was a scripture; I just let them think that I made it up (laughing out loud). That's not a sin; I didn't lie! I shared with them that some things of the past I just didn't have the desire to do anymore. Even though I stilled cussed and drank, God saved my soul; He didn't erase my memory. I still liked the taste of alcohol.

I guess basically what I was telling them was that, if I could come to church in an attempt to get my raggedy life together, then so could they. Coming to church was not about stopping old ways; it was about starting new ones. The starting would eventually lead to the stopping. When I went home that evening, I felt good, I felt smart, and I felt God was using me to reach those who I once sold drugs with, drank with, and partied with. Then it hit me like a ton of bricks! This is it God; this is my purpose; this is the plan that you have for my life. This is what you were telling me in the bathroom—to give to others what you had given me. To tell others my past and let them see what you had delivered me from; to give them hope. I got it! Now it's all starting to make sense. I recall reading a scripture one day that said, "And we know that all things work together for the good to them that love God, and are called according to His purpose (Romans 8:28).

I've got it; I've been called!

Chapter 7

Romans 8:28

❧❀☙

"And we know that all things work together for good to them that love God, to them who are the called according to *his* purpose" (Romans 8:28). My experience with God in the bathroom was his way of calling me to do ministry. And as the pastor had told me, what better person to use other than someone who had lived such a life as I had. Then I thought back on the things that I had been through, and began to pray, because although I had read the scripture and understood that I had been called into the ministry, I couldn't comprehend how it all was going to work out for my good. I understood how others could be helped. But how would it help me when it still hurt so badly? God said, "That's because you are looking at it from a place of pain; and, I'm looking at it as a tool for deliverance." He said, "I have set you free from the shame and embarrassment affiliated with the actions so that you may freely give your X- rated testimony, not the cute little one that you have been sharing in the grocery store and hair salon." He said, "It will work out for your good as soon as you begin to share your story. Your healing will begin as you start to minister to others because you will also be ministering to yourself." He said, "You have to stay encouraged, because a victory today does not guarantee a victory tomorrow."

So the day came ya'll when I was asked to speak a word of encouragement at my church to about 25 women. I wrote out my P.G. rated story and practiced it for about ten days before I was to present it. When the night came to speak, although I had my notes, God had me share events with them that I would have kept secret and quote scriptures that I didn't even know I knew. By the time I was finished, I had tears streaming down my face and they were all standing and crying also. When I took my seat, I couldn't even remember what I had said. I just knew that I was free! After the event, women were running up to me thanking me for sharing my story because many of them had been abused both physically and sexually and some had never even told anyone. But, after hearing me, they were ready to address their feelings and confront the perpetrator. I just hugged them and told them that God would give them the strength to deal with it and the wisdom of how to handle their situation. I was so proud of myself for letting God use me to help others.

On the way home, God whispered in my ear, "All things work together for the good." Then, I completely understood the scripture. So let me present it to you in a way in which I hope you can understand and gain wisdom from.

- Have you ever been bitter towards your parent(s) for things that happened to you while in their care?
- Have you ever been angry with a mate or a friend for the way they mistreated you?
- Have you ever been mad at yourself for allowing people and situations to control you?
- Have you ever been so far out there that you didn't think you could find your way to safety?
- Have you ever been upset with God for allowing terrible things to happen to you beyond your control?

If you have answered yes to any of these questions, let me present a truth that you need to treasure, a fact that you need to frame, and a principle that you need to ponder. And that is— no matter what happens in your life, God always acts in your best interest. Now you're asking, "What's my best interest?" It is anything that makes your life more like Jesus.

What I've come to understand is that before I knew Christ, everything that happened to me kept me feeling hopeless and helpless because I didn't understand why it was happening to me. However, I was asking the wrong question. It wasn't a matter of why, but a matter of what did God want me to learn. The Bible says that all things work for the good of those who love God. I loved God, but how could the abuse, hurt, and pain that I endured work for my good? Here's the good: if the bike had not fell on my head as a child, I would not have known that God was a healer. If Donna had not kicked up my plaid skirt, I would not know the seriousness behind bullying. If "the frog" had not slapped me in junior high, I wouldn't know teenage domestic violence existed. If I had not gotten the abortion, I would not have known that it's the actual death of a fetus and that it could have long-term effects of you never being able to conceive. Had I not nominated myself to be a drug dealer and party girl, I would have told my son that there is nothing in these streets. When in reality, there is a whole bunch of stuff in these streets and it all leads to jail or the cemetery. And my good list could go on and on, but the one I deem most important was the sexual abuse. Now you're wondering, *why that experience?* Because it was that experience that physically hurt the worst, the one that stills takes up space in my mind and the one in which I still frequently see the perpetrator. This is the cancer that has clogged up my arteries with bitterness, anger, and revengeful ways. This is the one that affects one out of every four women. This is also the one that caused me to run to Jesus. See before I knew Jesus, I didn't love him because I didn't know him. But he knew me; he knew what I would go through; and yet, he still had a plan for my life (Jeremiah 29:11). And although it didn't feel good, and at times it didn't look good, he was always working it out for my good. As I look back, I am able to see how it worked for my good. I am stronger; I am wiser. I am able to boldly and unashamedly speak of my tragedies. But mostly importantly, I know that God has called me for His purpose. And that is to encourage and uplift. I now realize that someone has to serve as a victim of abuse in order to stand as an ambassador for Christ. See, what I have learned is that it's not about what you have gone through in life; it's about what you have overcome.

Let me see if I can make this relevant to your life. In the Bible, in Luke chapter 22, verse 31, Jesus tells Simon that Satan has asked to sift you like wheat, meaning Satan is seeking permission to bring trouble to you. Now this might surprise some of you, but as a child of God, Satan has no control over your life unless you relinquish it to him. Everything that Satan brings up against you, God has already acknowledged that it's coming. To further prove my point, read the book of Job. But I want to shine the spot light on verse 32. Jesus says, "But I have prayed that your faith should not fail, so when you are converted, strengthen your brethren." Now had Jesus said "if" you are converted, I would have been worried, because it would have caused me to doubt His power, but "when" let's you know that no matter what you are going through that you are coming out. "When" let's you know that there is an expiration date to your trials. But that's not the end of it. There also comes a responsibility with deliverance. God is holding you responsible to not only testify of his goodness but to also be a resource of strength to others during their trials.

So after my sifting and conversion, I ran full speed telling people they needed to give their lives to Christ and trust God for everything—only to be disappointed. My enthusiasm was great, but God had to remind me that, "You are a resource of strength, not the source." My job was to simply present to them the tool (the Bible, His Word) that they needed to turn their lives around, not force it on them. So I understood that to mean that I was to give them the seed and what they chose to do with that seed was up to them. This also helped me to understand that some folk take longer to come around than others, and some would choose to never come out of their situation. I believe that my mom falls into one of these categories.

As I began to probe into my mother's childhood, I learned that she as a child and young adult had faced some very difficult situations also. She was extremely beautiful, had a nice voice, and was giving the opportunity to sing with a secular music group. However, her devoted, Christian mother denied her the experience. She got pregnant by the pastor's son at 18 and they publicly humiliated her by saying the baby wasn't his and put her out the church. When she went out, she vowed to never return and still hasn't till this day. Nine months later, she gave birth to twins and although they highly favored their dad, my mom was never given an apology from his family. She never had a relationship with her dad and never felt love by her mom. She, too, searched for love through relationships with men, which led to 9 kids with 5 baby daddies. In hearing the different stories of her past, I saw me. But not only did I see me, I also saw my other sisters. This, my friends, is what I would describe as a generational curse. We were all, in some way, living out my mom's past without any knowledge of it. This disease of unworthiness had gone undetected in her and we were all infected by it. When looking at this from a spiritual stand point, it allowed me to move from being angry with her to being empathetic with her. She simply did what she thought was best. And there was a good side; the man whom I thought was my dad, I soon learned had been sterile since a teenage boy, so he knew from day one that I wasn't his child and in spite of the lie, he still took good care of me and protected the lie that she portrayed until his death. The truth was finally revealed in his will. And as we read the will, my mom listened in a confused state and said, "Now why would your dad lie like that. I don't know what he is talking about." How she chooses and when she chooses to deal with the situations is up to her. My only responsibility is to give her the tool (the Bible, God's Word) and to never forget that just like she has faults, so do I. Believe me, if it had not been for the grace of God, I know exactly where I would be—dead! I believe that every time we saw my father that we saw a demonstration of God's love for this world—unconditional. And for that I am forever grateful to Elijah Henry; R.I.P., Dad.

Now I won't lie to you and say that I'm in a great place, but I will tell you that I am in a better place. Every day is a battle, but with the help of Jesus, I can win. And winning may not put you on a platform to receive a trophy, but it will put peace in your heart.

So I will quote the Apostle Paul in Philippians 3:12, "I don't mean to say that I have already achieved these things or that I have already reached perfection. But I press on to possess that perfection for which Christ Jesus first possessed me" (NLT).

In other words- I'm moving forward!

WHO IS ANDREA CLARK?

If there was one word to describe Andrea Clark it would be witty. After enduring trials and tribulations throughout her life thus far, she was prompted by the Holy Spirit to share her complicated testimonies through written words in hope of encouraging someone else. She speaks on issues such as Baby Mama Drama and Growing Pains which can be found within the chapters of Who Cried For The Little Girl. Her intriguing stories speak directly to those who are fighting within to make the correct choices in life. She shares how God delivered her from the pain of her past to a promising future.

Andrea was born and raised in Oakland, CA . She is the wife of Pastor Johnnie Clark Jr. The mother of two sons, Rodney Lampkin Jr. and Askari Goss and a proud grandmother. She has the awesome responsibilities of being a ordained minister and servant of God, daycare owner and foster parent for over 18 years, owner of Jesus Rock Christian apparel and accessories and now a author. Andrea began a real relationship with Christ in 1999 and has faithfully stayed in fellowship with her church. She founded and taught Women Walking In Wisdom home bible study for over 7 years. She has taken a vow through the aide of the Holy Spirit to be used by God as a vessel to encourage women from all walks of life. Because Andrea knows that if it had not been for the grace of God she would be dead. Her life long mission is to bring women together so they can work together to serve the Savior.